BEQUEATH

BEQUEATH

essays

Melora Wolff

LOUISIANA STATE UNIVERSITY PRESS
BATON ROUGE

Published by Louisiana State University Press
lsupress.org

LSU Press Paperback Original

DESIGNER: Michelle A. Neustrom
TYPEFACES: Tribute OT, display; Freight Text Pro, text

The content of this book is entirely the product of the author's
human memory and imagination.

COVER PHOTOGRAPH: iStockPhoto.com/CribbVisuals

LIBRARY OF CONGRESS CATALOGING-IN-PUBLICATION DATA
Names: Wolff, Melora, author.
Title: Bequeath : essays / Melora Wolff.
Description: Baton Rouge : Louisiana State University Press, 2024.
Identifiers: LCCN 2024010664 (print) | LCCN 2024010665 (ebook) |
    ISBN 978-0-8071-8277-2 (paperback) | ISBN 978-0-8071-8307-6 (pdf) |
    ISBN 978-0-8071-8306-9 (epub)
Subjects: LCGFT: Essays.
Classification: LCC PS3623.O5587 B47 2024 (print) | LCC PS3623.O5587
    (ebook) | DDC 814/.54—dc23/eng/20240511
LC record available at https://lccn.loc.gov/2024010664
LC ebook record available at https://lccn.loc.gov/2024010665

for my parents in memory
and to my family
present past future

I am to give you this
as you are leaving the garden

—W. S. MERWIN

Masters in This Hall 1

Fall of the Winter Palace 27

Poison Hour 49

Mystery Girls 71

Joy 95

End 111

How It Turned Out 119

Lost in Space 131

Bequeath 147

Begin 161

ACKNOWLEDGMENTS 167

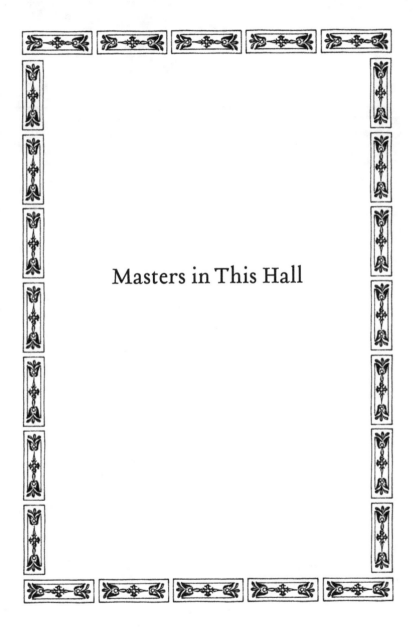

Masters in This Hall

WHO WERE THE FATHERS? We wanted to see them, to hear them—their coughs and quips, their songs and snorts, their belches and yawns, their whoops and rants—we wanted to hug them, to hug them all the time, to practice daily our hugging of fathers. Maybe we remembered hugging the fathers when we were little girls and they were like trees, and we balanced on the tops of their shoes; maybe we remembered lifting our arms above our heads and waiting for our fathers to lift us up as if we were little ballerinas, into the air where we spun and squealed; maybe we remembered climbing onto the broad backs of the fathers, hanging our tired selves around their shoulders and nodding to sleep, our saliva moistening their shirts while they kept walking through city parks; maybe we remembered lying on the pavement, knees skinned, trying hard not to look at the oozing blood because looking at blood— hadn't our fathers warned us?—would only make us cry. Maybe we had known we would always be alone with our torn knees and brimming tears until the fathers swept us up in their arms and carried us home, toward bandages and mothers' balms. Or maybe we remembered none of this at all. Maybe we wondered instead why we had never felt our fathers hugging us, why they always slipped away whenever we came near them, why they looked so very afraid.

Where were the fathers? They weren't in the lobby of the school. They weren't waiting to escort us beside the East River safely home. That was not the duty of the fathers, but of the unemployed mothers, who walked with us along the boardwalk, or under the school pier past the loiterers, the skateboarders and bikers, or across the busy New York City avenues. They listened to our descriptions of the school day. *We tied our belts together to look like Siamese twins! We flushed all the toilets at the same time! We saw Andy Warhol eating lunch in the cafeteria!* Yes, these were the details we told the weary mothers or sometimes the big sisters with their big-sister schoolbags slung over their shoulders, each bag emblazoned with the Brearley School's initials, "B.S." Some of the girls' mothers and big sisters never waited for them in the lobby after school at all—those girls had their own chauffeurs waiting for them, groomed and chunky guys the girls shouted out to warmly—"Buddy!" or "Rocky!"—as if the drivers were beagle pups or guppies. But we rarely saw the fathers who had made us. They appeared most often after dinner and just before bedtime, and we knew they would likely vanish again before sunrise. When they arrived home at dusk, they tugged at the ties around their throats; they dropped their overcoats, their briefcases or wallets, their typewriters or instruments with a loud thud in the dining rooms; they asked the mothers for a martini, an old-fashioned, or a scotch and soda. They sighed and draped their bodies across the furniture, like wide unfolded flags.

MANY YEARS AGO, the new young fathers had gathered in groups at birthday parties, where they wore golden construction paper crowns on their heads, scooped ice cream, and cut the purple cake. They had crawled on their hands and knees through the giant caterpillar Slinky and emerged glorious from the other side, their hands filled with costume jewelry. They had marched us through the halls to the big treasure chest with the padlock they broke open like a band of gruff pirates, and then tossed bracelets, bangles, necklaces, and chocolate coins into the air for us to gather up in our party skirts. They helped us beat the piñata to shreds with tennis rackets, and we had all cheered together. So, the fathers were persuaded to show up years later at the Gold and Silver Balls—the cotillions held in the school auditorium—where they leaned silently against the walls as our chaperones. The cotillions were always controlled, proper, and festooned. There was hot tea and a platter of donuts. There were no boy bands singing in falsettos, only Simon and Garfunkel harmonizing on the loudspeakers, "I Am a Rock." Peripheral, the fathers slouched in their nostalgia while we danced around them in our patent leather high heels. They appeared lost and sad. Although the cotillions were nothing like the musky dances held over at the boys' school, we knew that these moping fathers were nevertheless *necessary* as our witnesses—to preserve decorum, to defend our girlish decency, and to beat back predators as if they were piñatas.

Above the heads of the fathers gathered vigilantly in the auditorium loomed the portraits of the heads of school for the past century. First were the older portraits of the masters, beginning of course with the school's founding father, Samuel Brearley. In his portrait, Samuel wore nineteenth-century clothing and had long curled hair like a girl. Skeptics, who opposed the intellectual and social advancement of young girls, had asked Samuel, "Will education remove the blush from the girls' cheeks?" "No, it will not!" our founding father Samuel had decreed. He delivered lectures on education for women; he answered questions; he asked for further financial support; everywhere, he promoted and publicized his newly founded girls' school. After Samuel's sudden death from typhoid, another man became master of the school, and when that master died quickly, as though some supernatural office disapproved of masters in schools of girls, the heads that succeeded the two men were women: dour, sturdy, and imposing. The headmistresses lived long lives. They posed for their portraits in black robes. Oily and solemn, they gazed out years later at all these blushing, coltish girls and looked embarrassed for us. The fathers stood beneath these lady-portraits and watched us twirl in our dotted Swiss dresses the mothers had selected, though we preferred the silk shifts with spaghetti straps the girls with breasts wore in the Upper School. The fathers breathed in our Middle School breezes of tea-rose perfume; they glanced at our bodies, spindly and coiffed in the arms of panic-stricken boys. The fathers looked proud, embarrassed, violent, tender, fierce, exhausted, indifferent, curious, covetous, competitive, loving, amused, and mean. They lowered their eyes as we went past them. They whispered to each other every now and then and burst into very loud laughter. Sometimes, they slapped each other hard on the back or shoulder. Sometimes they held out pale sticks of gum to one another. The fathers chewed gum as if it were pieces of raw flesh, their mouths moist and open.

WE LAUNCHED AN enthusiastic campaign, inviting as many fathers as possible to visit our classes and tell us about their jobs—regardless of their line of work—so that we could stare at them. While the fathers described their jobs, we were able to study the men themselves, like a new and foreign subject in our classrooms. We could admire their long legs—elegantly and professionally crossed—the cashmere of their suits, the gleam of their freshly shaven faces, the stray locks of their combed hair slipping boyishly across their foreheads as they spoke. Amazing, we thought, that the fathers could look so much like boys; amazing that this was so very appealing, whereas boys never looked at all like fathers and were never appealing. We were also amazed to gain the fathers' intimate insider perspectives on their work. From the obliging fathers, we learned about architecture, screen-writing, white-water rafting, neurology, symphony performance, opera, podiatry, campaign management, newspaper journalism, painting, banking, publishing, composing, aircraft control, television production, jazz, gynecology, and the Supreme Court. Lena's father demonstrated the candy dispenser he had invented, a plastic stick with a smiling head on the top. If you twisted the head, a pink candy spurted out. Sarah's father, the architect, took us on a tour of Times Square, pointing to all of the buildings he had designed.

"That big tall one over there," he said as we hurried behind him with our teacher, Miss Dunn, "I designed that one—and that one too. You should see it at night. It lights up. It's something."

We attracted a certain attention that day—the sharp, sleek father and his coterie of girls in matching uniforms, socks, and wool jackets with B.S. insignias, marching beneath red, neon, flashing marquees and past clusters of older women wearing wigs, heavy makeup, and matching outfits of their own. Some of the ladies smiled at us. Others did not. Miss Dunn said she was feeling dizzy, and so we all headed back to the school without finishing the architectural tour. We didn't mind. We thought the buildings Sarah's father had created all looked exactly the same, completely boring, but we said nothing to him, as he was sweating and seemed exhausted by his abbreviated tour.

IN THE AFTERNOON, we trained in gym class where we yelled and shoved each other, divided into two furious teams, the Reds and the Whites. When the weather was good, the Reds and Whites trained on the securely wire-fenced pier above the river. We had a fleeting audience of rakish-looking men, sailors on the decks of boats gliding by the school. "Hoa, girls!" the sailors shouted and whooped. "Throw that ball over here! Why don't you come away with us?" and they waved their arms as they passed.

Our sport was blitzkrieg, which was actually dodgeball, but the lady gym teachers preferred the name blitzkrieg. Dodgeball was for losers. Blitzkrieg was for leaders. We flung the hard, pink balls deliriously at each other with a force that sent many girls crying to Nurse. The school nurse had been the inspiration for a classic black-and-white film made in the 1950s, a dramatic depiction of her own youthful wedding called *Father of the Bride*. In the film, our school nurse was played by the most beautiful and glamorous of women, Elizabeth Taylor, which we found both impressive and unbelievable, because the nurse bore no resemblance whatsoever to Elizabeth Taylor: she was gray-haired and wore white orthopedic shoes, a little white cap, horn-rimmed glasses, and white knee socks. She had a general aura not of femininity, but of anonymity and resignation. In the film, our nurse's father was played by Spencer Tracy. When we had all gathered in Heather's living room to watch a reel-to-reel film of *Father of the Bride*, we laughed at Spencer Tracy looking robust and peeved as he struggled into his cutaway tuxedo for his daughter's wedding day. "You have a little girl," Tracy lamented to his fellow fathers, "You're her Oracle. You're her hero. And then the day comes . . ." From Tracy we understood that a handsome, flustered father may grieve when his daughter leaves him for another man.

Battered and ambitious, we blitzkrieg soldiers staggered from gym class with our bloody noses to the Hollywood nurse's clinic, where we lay on her medical cots moaning like the Civil War amputees in *Gone with the Wind*. We asked her questions about Spencer Tracy. We asked her about beautiful weddings, jewelry, and expensive bridal gowns. She applied spoons to our necks to stop the bleeding of our injured noses. She said she did not know Spencer Tracy, and she definitely did not approve of young ladies playing blitzkrieg, but we assured her bloody injury was our badge of honor. The Whites were winners! The Reds were losers. Both of the teams were better than the boys' teams, we told Nurse; we were smarter and tougher, and she sighed and said, yes, we were tough girls, very tough. Then she adjusted our ponytails and sent us back into the drama of the battle.

Sometimes we gathered at the Collegiate boys' school gym across town, to watch the really fit boys sweat, and to admire their speed, their new muscles, and their remarkable knees. The boys' gym stank of their sweat and dank T-shirts. The old heating pipes clanked above the court as the boys ran like demons, shoving and shouting. This was not unlike our own gym classes. We cheered the boys, half-heartedly, at their games. We knew that those sweaty boys weren't the *real* males; they were just the *miniatures*, many of them with noses that bled suddenly during conversation with girls at the Gaiety Mixers, without any blitzkrieg injury at all. The boys' noses just spontaneously ejaculated blood down their shirt fronts, and they wiped the blood away with the back of their hands and kept trying to talk to us, pretending nothing had happened at all, pretending their shirts weren't soaked. They looked like they'd been stabbed. Their voices cracked and groaned. They had a rowdy humor that made us shudder. The jocks pounding past us at the basketball games were the same boys that threw each other around for hours on rubber mats after school, a coach screaming in their ears, *pound harder!* They lost their teeth and didn't mind. They broke their whole faces and didn't mind. They limped and spit. They burped and stretched. They grinned too much too.

But what would happen after that? After they grew older? Could any one of them ever earn our love and respect or Spencer Tracy's wrath? We cheered whenever a tall boy dunked the ball through the net with impeccable force and scored, but we didn't really care. Our determined lady teachers—all of them impressive—had taught us girls emphatically: women are *essential*; men are just *inevitable*. We were taught never to forget that. Women, they said, would build the world! Men would just live in it. It was 1972.

WE ALL PRESSURED Sue to invite her father to visit the school, because she had told us once, very casually, that her father was an actor and had a role on *The Mod Squad*. But she wouldn't invite him to come to our school so we never believed she was telling the truth about his profession, until one afternoon her mother failed to appear in the lobby, and Sue's father was summoned at once by the American history teacher. Girls started to gather in the school lobby at 2:30 p.m. We chatted in little cliques, hoping to see Sue's father when he arrived. Some teachers gathered too, over by the coat-check room where they kept a low profile. At 3:05, Mod Squad Dad sauntered into the lobby, his dark glasses perched on the end of his nose, and his jeans slung low on his hips. He lit a cigarette. Who would tell this father that he could not smoke his Marlboros in the lobby of the girls' school? While he waited for Sue to collect her books and gym bag, he read the notices pasted around the elevator, performing his deep interest in the new Latin Club, in the publicity posters for our all-girl production of *The Importance of Being Earnest*, and in the audition announcements for our exciting upcoming coed production of *West Side Story*, which we would produce with the boys' school. We had selected *West Side Story* as our coed show because Nina's father had composed the music for it and one day actually had played "I Feel Pretty" for us on his own grand piano—and a few chords too of "A Boy Like That" until we accidentally tipped a giant library ladder over on top of him and smashed his music rack. We were impressed by his good nature about this incident. Our poster for *West Side Story* featured an illustration of boys at the rumble—the Jets and the Sharks—waving big knives, with a fuzzy-looking Maria weeping in the background. Mod Squad Dad soon lost interest in our poster board. He unzipped his black leather jacket. He had a sexy gap between his teeth. When Sue arrived, he whistled through the gap like the start of an excellent musical over-ture. We pretended not to care when Sue kissed his cheek and he lifted her, briefly, off the floor. Enviously, we watched Sue swing out the glass doors of the school with her groovy, crime-busting dad.

IN THE LATE-AUTUMN AFTERNOONS, we practiced for the Christ-mas Assembly. We worked for several months to perfect the program. All of the parents attended the annual Christmas Assembly in Assembly Hall, the mothers seated in the upper balcony as queens might be seated, and the fathers seated in the lower darkness beneath the balcony, like galley slaves. The mothers would wear bright, silken dresses for this occasion, beautiful fox and mink and rabbit fur coats they would drape over the edge of the balcony railing, and the fathers wore vests and dark suits, so that no father's individual identity could be easily discerned in the ocean of men at the back of the hall. One or two fathers might be wearing garish neckties, or have scarlet handkerchiefs folded into their breast pockets, and a few might have wind-blown hair that made them look more like characters from Dr. Seuss than like fathers, but most of the fathers were undistinguished. Or rather, all of the fathers were distinguished, and therefore, they were indistinguishable from one another.

The girls' chorus was disciplined to gather beneath the portraits of the founding father and headmaster, Samuel, and of the other master and headmistresses. The chorus would then lead all of the classes and visiting parents in a medley of carols our music teacher, Miss Haven, had selected for us, including "We Three Kings," "God Rest Ye Merry Gentlemen," "Little Drummer Boy," "Rudolph the Red-Nosed Reindeer," and "Good King Wenceslas." The fathers would sing the part of the Good King, and we girls would sing the part of the king's page. We also learned the French carol that would accompany our entrance to the hall. Miss Haven said this was a seventeenth-century tune originally called "The Female Sailor" until, that is, some ambitious man had changed its title. We learned a jazz carol called "Shepherd's Pipe Carol"—which allowed Leslie to play a solo on her violin, although it was not a pipe—and finally a strange minor-key song Miss Haven called a lively holiday anomaly, about a Spartan boy who was bitten to death by a fox he kept hidden inside his coat. Why, we wondered, didn't the Spartan boy scream if his fox was biting him to death? Why didn't he keep his fox somewhere else, like in a cage or a box? Katie said this must be a cautionary song about male masturbation. As editor in chief of the girls' school literary magazine, *The Beaver*, Katie was an expert in metaphors, but even she conceded that the lyric was inscrutable. Would Miss Haven pick a male masturbation song for the Christmas Assembly? It seemed unlikely. The chorus of the song went, "So he dropped down dead-a-dead-a-dead all dead but ripe for glory." This sentiment, whatever its meaning, seemed best suited for the *beginning* of the Christmas program, as a warm-up of sorts, before we gathered steam with "Here Comes Santa Claus."

The altos were to stand on the left side of the chorus, the sopranos on the right, the soloists in the center, and the bell carriers in the front of the soloists, poised for the ringing of the bells. I was the low D bell.

We bell carriers were to hold our bells resting against our shoulders like small babies we were about to burp, and when our note approached, we were to lift the bell gently from our shoulder, and then, at just the right moment, plunge the bell fiercely downward as though we were hurling the baby to the floor with a wrenching thrust of the arm. The pain of this motion is known only to bell ringers and parachutists. After our bell had resonated fully, we were to return the bell in a smooth gliding motion to our shoulder. As difficult as we found it to be the bell ringers, we also knew we fourteen girls had been granted an absolute honor: to lead the entire school, and the mothers and the fathers in rejoicing. Because of the bell ringers, Christmas would sound as the ancients had intended it to sound when they first filled the air with the echoing of bells and song and sweet voices raised on high, heralding the birth of Jesus, the Holy Son of God, the Blessed Father.

WE DOUBTED THAT any father would impress us as much as Sue's *Mod Squad* father, until Mimi's father visited our class. Mimi's father was a gynecologist. On the day he visited, he stood confidently at the front of the room in front of the blackboard, his hands on his hips as he faced some thirty of us in our jumpers and doily-collared blouses. Behind him blazed the single word he had written on the blackboard like the opening title of a television detective show, "Spermicide." We waited uneasily for his insights. Our homeroom teacher, Mademoiselle France, also looked uneasy in her place behind the front desk.

"Girls," he said, "I know you're just twelve. But you should all get yourselves diaphragms. So when you have sex you won't get pregnant and ruin your lives. Getting pregnant doesn't automatically ruin your life. That's not my point. But if you're pregnant and you're twelve, well, I don't care what those girls did back on the prairie in the olden days. We aren't on the prairie. We're in New York City. I know some of you are having sex, right?"

Nobody spoke. Was Mimi having sex? Or did he mean someone else? Was he just guessing?

"Well," he went on, "I know some of you are. And I think that's *terrific*. Sex is *terrific*. You should all know that. It's my job to tell you that."

This seemed like an unusual job, but we were intrigued.

"So, if you've never seen a diaphragm before," he continued, "it looks like this." He reached over to the teacher's desk and grabbed Mademoiselle France's silver desk bell, which he waved above his head. "A diaphragm looks like this. Except it doesn't have a bell. It doesn't ever ring. And you can fold a diaphragm in half, but this thing is made of metal, so they're different in those ways. A diaphragm isn't made of metal. It's made of latex. Otherwise, they're the same. But don't mess around with this thing"—he dinged the bell—"because *ouch*. You get the idea. Do you have any questions?"

Was it possible that anyone had a question? Mademoiselle France looked pale. A hand shot up. It was Madeleine. We had long suspected Madeleine hoped to have something close to sex during lunch break with the drama teacher, a very young fellow just graduated from Vassar whom we all called contemptuously by his first name, Eddie.

"Do you like having sex?" Madeleine called to Mimi's father loudly from the back of the room.

We all sank lower in our seats.

Mademoiselle France said, "I'm afraid we're all out of time, but this has been terrific—not *terrific*—but informative and so useful."

"I love having sex!" Mimi's father bellowed. "It's my job to tell you that!"

IN LATIN CLASS, we had completed our translations of *Julia*, a short book about a little girl who walks by the sea and tries to learn the history of Greece and Rome, just as we all tried to translate *Julia* from Latin to English, so that her story could become even less interesting. When we had finished translating *Julia,* we remembered only the opening sentence, *Iulia puella parva est*—"Julia is a little girl." We were excited to embark next on a translation of *The Aeneid.* Madame Kotke paced at the front of the room in her black dress and oxford shoes, proclaiming *The Aeneid*'s dramatic opening sentence, "*arma virumque cano!*" and we chanted back, "I sing of arms and the man!" Madame helped us through pages of the hero's battles in the Trojan War, the advance of the Trojan Horse, and of the returning warriors' funeral games. Aeneus pleased us as much as Miranda and her dethroned father, Prospero, in exile together on an island in *The Tempest,* and as much as the feuding Montagues and Capulets in *Romeo and Juliet,* plays we studied with Miss Wright in English. When Heather failed to bring her copy of *The Aeneid* to Latin class, Madame Kotke said fiercely, "Heather, you remind me of the potato fields!"

Many years ago, Madame was a little girl—as little as Julia, she emphasized—and lived on a farm with her father and brothers five miles from the fields where men dug potatoes. She begged the men to let her dig potatoes. One dark morning, Madame reported, her father allowed her to walk the five miles to dig potatoes with the men. But when she arrived at the potato field, she saw she had forgotten to bring her shovel. She walked the long way back alone. "And what is the moral of this story?" Madame demanded of Heather.

"Don't live on a farm," Heather said.

"Eat rice," Katie tried.

"If you want to work alongside men," Madame shouted, as though she might melt, "you must be prepared, girls! You must bring your tools! Men will not help you, they will only laugh! You cannot dig potatoes if you do not bring your shovel!"

We nodded. We wrote this moral in our notebooks between *Iulia puella parva est* and *arma virumque cano.*

* * *

ONCE, A FATHER APPEARED abruptly in our classroom and removed a daughter by force. He offered no apology. He gave no explanation. The air in the classroom went still, a silence fell, and Mademoiselle France changed the subject quickly as the door slammed after the father and the stumbling girl. She was that girl who never spoke. She wasn't like the rest of us, with our shiny long hair twirled in buns and braids and ponytails. She was the one who wore black eyeliner, kept her gaze on the floor, and wore her hair very short. She kept her shoulders rounded, and she had pierced her nose five times. She was a real talent on the guitar, a star. She played her guitar every afternoon out by the lockers at recess, and her lonesome wails echoed. She scared us all. She was a dark wave that rolled through the hallways of the school, drowning everyone in her path. In our new and progressive psychology class, the peppy play therapy teacher, with the turquoise earrings and tie-dyed skirt who told us all to call her "Miss Julie," asked us all to build "environments" we dreamed of, out of potted plants and blocks and plastic dolls she distributed to us all like blank checks, which we would have preferred.

"Dolls?" the shadow girl snorted.

I shrugged and stripped all my dolls. Slowly, I worked on making a tribal jungle village on the banks of the Amazon River. I arranged some naked natives launching a raft I made out of a short wood ruler, on which I laid a maiden bound by rubber bands. But the shadow girl worked very quickly. She built a massive medieval fortress, fortified with high walls, a blue yarn moat, and a large forest of ivy plants and jade. She placed paper clip catapults along the block walls.

"Why isn't there a drawbridge for the fortress," Miss Julie asked, "so people can get inside?"

"Because they don't want anyone to get inside," the girl said.

"Who are they keeping out?" There was a slight tremor in Miss Julie's voice.

The girl stared at her, and then said flatly, "The Army of Fathers."

IN HISTORY CLASS, Miss Nestle scheduled movies about the Second World War. Several of the fathers had served in one war, or another, Miss Nestle said, and although she herself had never seen any of our fathers except at the parent-teacher meetings, where they sat silently behind the mothers until money was mentioned, she said they were all heroes. Katie said she thought Hilary's father must still be depressed from the war in Korea. She had glimpsed him during her sleepover visits to Hilary's. He lay curled up in a tight ball on a tiny threadbare love seat beneath a painting of the sea, not moving. He had wrapped himself inside a newspaper as if it were a blanket, and clutched the pages of news about Vietnam inside his fists as he slept. He wouldn't get up. He didn't seem to have a job. "Something wasn't right with him," Katie said. "A father shouldn't sleep like a homeless man in newspapers on a tiny love seat. He looks like a big shrimp in a cocktail, or a dead baby in a box."

We wanted to believe Miss Nestle when she said the fathers were heroes, even though we knew she had certainly never seen the fathers in the kitchen late at night, making peanut butter sandwiches; she had never spied on them spinning the dials around and around on the radio in the dark morning, listening to bursts of music and static; she had never seen them hanging a door poorly on its hinge, or scouring a burned frying pan, or trying to give water to a baby guinea pig with a syringe. She would not have been able to imagine these unlikely acts of heroism, just as we were not able to imagine—never *wanted* to imagine—the fathers with guns, with grenades, with backpacks, and with bullets on their belts.

We had seen no photographs of the fathers in Germany, or in Korea. In our dreams, even the fathers' faces remained shaded under helmets so that we could not see their eyes, and their boy-soldier bodies crawled through mud toward some enemy, or dozed restlessly and anonymously in shadows on bedrolls, in the backs of covered trucks, in dirt, or in trenches. Perhaps the fathers had dreamed of their unborn daughters then, just as we dreamed of our fathers now. Or maybe they dreamed they would never have daughters at all, only sons that would beget more sons that would beget more sons. Maybe they prayed to God they would never have children at all.

On a Friday Film Day, Miss Nestle announced that there would be an afternoon screening of *The Twisted Cross* for anyone who was interested. After lunch, we all gathered on blankets on the history classroom floor to watch Hitler rise to power. Miss Jones—the woodshop and pottery teacher—arrived unexpectedly for the screening. Downstairs in the shop, Miss Jones had taught us all how to swing a hammer, how to use a table saw, how to build benches and shellac bookshelves. She had taught us how to heat the massive black kiln and bake our pottery cups and bowls inside, and how to glaze them to perfection when, finally, we removed them from the oven. We wouldn't need a man, she said, to build our houses or put food on our tables! We girls would build the world! We were the future! She strode into the room on *The Twisted Cross* day covered in sawdust, with her lunch in a paper bag. She pulled up a chair, and joined our audience. She was in a good mood, a fine mood, a *movie-going* mood. She was ready, she said, to see Hitler again. Miss Jones said, "Girls, you don't know what Hitler meant for us then, for all the Youth. He was so charismatic. He was so handsome, so strong! He was the father some of us had never had."

Our education had not prepared us to consider Hitler as our pottery teacher's father. We simply watched as Miss Nestle hurried to the light switch. She tripped on a blanket in the dark. She told us the film was broken, our screening of *The Twisted Cross* was canceled. She apologized. Miss Jones tossed her apple core into the trash can and left. Two days later, the rumors began. The teachers whispered. The big sisters whispered. Discreetly, the fathers had formed a chain of command. They had left their work; they had hurried at dusk in a rainstorm; they had gathered in the lobby of the school, stomped rain from their boots; they had walked together through the halls to the headmistress's office. The fathers spoke their piece, and in a sudden flash, Miss Jones was gone, as though she had never shellacked a shelf or baked a bowl—as though she had never existed. None of us saw her extinguished. Maybe it never happened. Maybe I write to command the army of the fathers.

WHEN MISSY'S FATHER had completed his Erhard Seminars Training, he allowed a few of us to visit his art studio to see his latest paintings. After his e.s.t., he said, he decided to work on a new series of paintings, each one with a black background, and with bright flowers depicted at the center of each canvas. So far, he had painted chrysanthemums, roses, sunflowers, irises, baby's breath, pansies, day lilies, and gardenias. He propped each canvas against the wall so that we might study the colors, and the three-dimensional effects he had achieved. He said that after he completed his e.s.t., beauty meant more to him than before. He had discovered a place of silence at the center of his being that was filled with flowers. He had freed himself from his base desires, from his impulses of rage and violence and from the urge to control other human beings. He had discovered Peace. He was in command of Serenity. During e.s.t, he said, everyone had been locked into a large room, and no one was allowed to leave until they had met their inner selves and taken control of their impulses.

"How did you go to the bathroom?" Katie asked Missy's father.

He said, "We didn't go to the bathroom, Katie, we had to stay locked inside the room until we completed our e.s.t. We controlled our bodily needs. We didn't go to the bathroom. We were locked in the large room. We stayed there. We met our inner selves. We made drawings. Look," he said, and he gave each of us a small blank index card with a curved line drawn on it. "Do you girls know what this curved line represents? Can you complete this drawing?"

Missy's father waited while we each drew a picture on our index card, incorporating the strange curved line into our own imaginative scenes. I drew a tiny man staring up at a leafy tree. Katie drew a pregnant owl sitting on a branch. She gave the owl a caption balloon, in which she wrote the word "Who?"

Missy's father collected our pictures and nodded. "Yes," he said, "these drawings reveal your budding sexual natures, and my paintings reveal—" He held above his head a large, terrific painting of drooped flowers. Secretly we wondered, what would Mimi's father say?

ANOTHER FATHER—my father—had also been in the war, in Germany. I knew for a fact that my father did not sleep on a sofa inside the daily news of Vietnam, and when I stayed up late one night to tell him we had studied wars, the assassination of Archduke Ferdinand, the Western Front, invasions, camps, and exterminations, he agreed reluctantly to visit our history class. He arrived in khaki trousers, a wool sweater, and sneakers. Miss Nestle greeted him warmly and offered him a desk-chair at the front of the room.

"Tell us whatever you remember," Miss Nestle said encouragingly, and added, "Anything. We know you were a very young man, just a little older than the girls are now."

My father folded himself awkwardly into the desk chair and looked at all our faces without saying anything. The air was tense. I feared my father would fail his classroom visit. Then, he described the beautiful countryside in Germany. He described long roads unwinding like velvet ribbons, and convoys of trucks rolling over the hills in darkness. He described nights without moonlight, an abandoned manor balanced like a jewel on a cliff, and how the men in his unit curled on its marble floor until dawn, breath held and waiting. He described music rising among the trees. He said there were unfamiliar smells wafting over the fields on a wind. He said if we were careful he would show us an object he had discovered in Dachau during the last days of the war, after the liberations—a golden knife with a porcelain handle. We passed this knife carefully around the room, and studied the nearly illegible signature engraved on the handle: *Adolf Hitler*. We sat very still. Miss Nestle returned the knife to my father, and I saw she did not touch the signature. My father said he still had dreams about the war, and suddenly I knew this for a fact too, because each night, I heard him through the bedroom walls of our city apartment, shouting and moaning like a little boy in his sleep, and I plugged my ears trying not to listen. He told us all his dreams were gray, and that sometimes it was very hard for him to wake up from his dreams. Many girls exchanged a glance, maybe thinking of Hilary's father still asleep on the threadbare love seat. I stared at my father's sneakers as though I'd never seen them before. His laces were untied.

OUR COED "INTERSCHOOL" production of *West Side Story,* which we would perform in the week preceding the Christmas Assembly, featured more girls than boys, because few boys auditioned and only a few of these boys would pass as gang members. Some resembled Jets, but none of them looked like Sharks. There was a boy with hunched shoulders and square hips who kept a damp cigarette he never smoked between his lips; there was a boy with pale wrists who avoided all of the girls; there was a boy with gold chains around his neck; a reptilian boy with a mermaid tattooed on his shoulder; a boy with glasses larger than his face; and the boy with the rust-red moustache. These boys were cast as the Jets. The four boys cast as Sharks were all named Dan. There was no explanation for this. Our musical director Miss Rose signaled to us to practice our Act I finale. We stood in our knee socks, blouses, and gym shorts and piped "Tonight" in five-part chorus with the Jets and the Dans. We tried to rock it. We tried to have us a ball.

"No girls! You're angry!" Miss Rose shouted at us. "Let me hear Anger!

You live on the streets! Your parents don't love you! You're angry West Side misfits!"

We rehearsed the rumble, and the deaths: Bernardo killed Riff; Tony killed Bernardo; Chino killed Tony. A freckled boy we had never seen before played the sniper Chino. Song and dance and knives and guns made men of all the boys. We watched them spin with a natural grace unavailable to those jocks we had seen pounding each other on rubber mats at the boys' school gymnasium. These agile theater boys threw each other to the floor like pros. They rolled and jumped to the music Nina's father had composed. They *lunged*. We were pleased to see they *dodged*. Sometimes they smiled. When the boys stepped offstage, they handed each other sticks of gum and slapped each other on the back. In stage makeup, they all looked older; in stage light, they all looked handsome. Lisa held DJ's sweaty hand, and whispered, like a Capulet, "Don't tell my father, he'll kill you"; then Sylvia held Paul's sweaty hand and whispered, "Don't tell my father, he'll kill you"; then Mimi kissed Roger; Lee kissed Dan; Katie kissed Dan; Jen kissed Dan; Liz kissed Jack; Katie kissed Bill; Elaine kissed Jay; Missy kissed Jimmy; I kissed Tony. We kissed and kissed, with lyrics in our heads that promised not just any night. We sang of love and arms and men. We pictured our fathers beating all these beautiful boys to death with tennis rackets. We pictured our fathers looking sadly into the camera, just like Spencer Tracy.

Our lips still aching, we gathered onstage with the boys around the fallen body of Tony, for the funereal end of the show. The boys hung their heads; the girls pretended to sob. We draped a black veil over the face of the girl who played Maria. Then, the Jets and the Dans struggled to lift the body of Tony onto their shoulders, and they carried him away beneath the blue lights, past the carefully designed set of wire fences and into the blackness of the wings where they dropped him, and he got back to his feet. Mr. Foote, our piano player, rang the minor chords of the final dirge.

WE KNEW OF only one girl among us whose father had actually died. She was small when it happened. She was a little girl. Clearly, this girl's oracle was nothing like our own, but perpetual, and all-powerful in his planetary silence. She was that older girl with the straight brown hair, always brushed, and with the pale brows and solemn eyes. She had a tender glance for each of us; she never looked away. We did not expect such a glance from a girl who had lost her father—as though she worried for us all, or knew she was gazing at us from an isolated galaxy we would someday occupy ourselves. She walked with a straight and dignified posture, her schoolbooks balanced on her arm, and when she passed us in the hallways, we stepped aside for her and did not know what to say. There was nothing we could say. We felt awe when we saw her. We felt hot shame. We felt a distant, intimate anguish that made us turn from her and then look back. Her father was gone yet she continued to live. His sudden death was a violation of a natural order. How would she be a daughter without her father? We felt we knew this girl's father, even, perhaps, that we loved him, although we had only heard about him, from our mothers, from our fathers too, and we had read about him in archived newspapers and in our American history books. Everyone mourned her father, who had been killed by a sniper on a November day in Dallas when our lives had barely begun.

Did the fathers weep? Did they close the doors and lower themselves, broken, into chairs? Did they wipe the palm of their hands across their faces, and feel ashamed of their weeping, and frightened by it, and yet surrender to their sobs like boys whose hearts have been permanently broken? Did they try to clear their throats and smooth their hair and adjust their neutral gaze before stepping again into the stoic world of still-living fathers? We knew that many of the fathers did cry, quietly, invisibly, in secret locked rooms we would never dare enter. We imagined their shoulders trembling, their arms folded across their stomachs, their bodies torn with an unfathomable pain they kept concealed inside their coats. We imagined those fathers who, in some other catastrophic disruption of the natural order, had survived their own daughters, for a few schoolgirls among us were gone, without any explanation: the girl who fell headfirst down the slope of ice, her skis and legs tangled; the girl who took a shortcut down a dark alley; the girl whose body folded slowly into paralysis; the girl who had a tumor; the girl hit by a car on a quiet street; the girl who left and didn't leave a note; the girl who glided like the dead through rooms; and the girls—too many of us girls—who starved for no apparent purpose, like prisoners of a war we could not name, our breasts shrinking, our hair falling out like fairy dust, our hips bending like carved bowls, our twelve ribs piercing our own flesh like blades.

ON THE DAY of the Christmas Assembly, we wore our crisply laundered uniforms and marched in perfect rank and file beneath the school flag. We marched past the elevators, past the cafeteria, and past the restrooms. We could hear the music teachers Miss Haven and Miss Rose and Miss Nives and the school orchestra already playing Christmas carols on their violins and cellos, setting the holiday mood. We heard the warbling voices of all the elegant mothers already seated in the balcony, talking, anticipating our carefully choreographed arrival. We spotted the school nurse. She was not wearing her white cap, or a bridal gown, but a fashionable and feminine lace dress and high heels. She looked elegant. We entered Assembly Hall through the four open arched doorways, and saw the welcoming golden light of the hall, the stage decked with smaller holiday bulbs, the wooden stairs where the chorus would gather, and the large metal rack that held all of the bells we would soon ring in joyful noise. We saw the podium where the headmistress would deliver her Christmas speech heralding a shifting world, a new world built by the smart young girls gathered before her. We saw too, one after another, the faces of the headmistresses staring blankly at us from their portraits as they had stared through a century of Christmas Assemblies, and the faces of the two fallen headmasters, ending with Samuel, our founding father, who looked approving.

The smallest and youngest girls led us into the Hall beneath Samuel's portrait. The fifth-graders were followed by the sixth-graders, then by the sevenths, the eighths, and once we girls had all gathered nervously in front of our chairs, we awaited the entrance of the fathers. They would follow behind us, marching to their places beneath the balcony. Then, we would sing.

We could see the fathers standing in the hallway, waiting to march. Every girl tried to glimpse her own father, but they had become one river of blue suits, no man independent of another. They all looked the same. The fathers jostled each other. They smoothed their hair. They adjusted kerchiefs in their pockets. They shuffled through the pages of their lyrics, and dropped pages onto the floor without noticing. We could hear them clearing their throats, too. They made phlegmy hacking sounds. There were a few short bursts of laughter from the unruly fathers, followed by the shushing sounds of the disciplined fathers. We heard the sound of their dress shoes scraping on the tiled floor. We had never seen so many men's polished dress shoes! Then Mr. Foote began pounding out the chords of the seventeenth-century French carol we had rehearsed. The descending chords of this obscure carol were the fathers' signal to enter the Hall.

As the fathers moved forward, we noted with some amazement that they walked very clumsily, as though they did not know how to march in rhythm at all, and that they strayed from their formation and bumped into one another. A few times they completely stalled, as though they were in traffic. Metal chairs scraped and clattered, and the fathers finally came to a discombobulated halt. Miss Haven stood at the front of the Hall, facing the fathers, eyeing them grimly. They quieted down. Her expression remained stern and forgiving. She raised her baton to signal the start of the Assembly, the entrance chords reached a crescendo, and, in one booming voice that echoed between the walls of portraits, the chorus of fathers sang out:

> Masters in this Hall
> Hear ye news today!
> Brought from over sea
> And ever I you pray!

There was a ripple of laughter from the girls. We had never heard such a strange sound in our own girls' school Assembly Hall, the sound of one hundred and seventy-five fathers singing together—the impossibly thunderous voices of the fathers who had backed away when we were born, afraid of holding us, afraid of dropping us, afraid of teaching daughters; fathers who had carried us, and knelt beside us, and pressed our first glass of champagne to our lips; heroes who had lifted us onto the carousel and watched us shout and ride our wooden horses in a harmless cavalry; fathers who knew everything and nothing about us, who loved us too little and too much; oracles who became rocks, and islands, and ghosts; fathers who closed their doors or flew into the clouds or looked into the camera or looked away; men who had all, so far, survived themselves.

> Christ the Lord is born,
> Masters be ye glad!
> Christmas is come in,
> And no folk should be sad!
> Nowell! Nowell! Nowell!
> Nowell sing we clear!

Holpen are all folk on earth,
Born is God's Son so dear!

We knew in our bones, this was a sound—like the rumbles of a shifting earth—we would never hear again. In our strongest voice, we sang with our fathers.

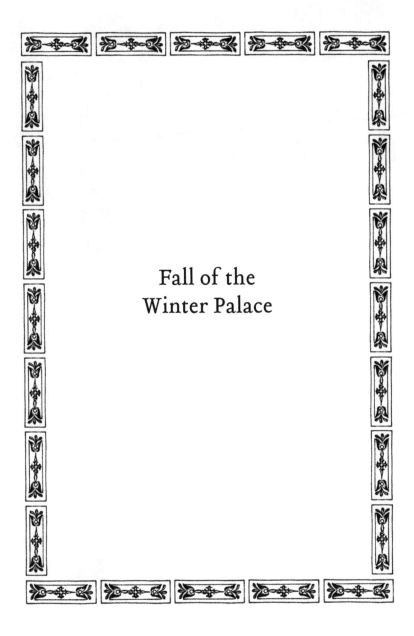

Fall of the
Winter Palace

K ERENSKY, RUMOR HAD IT, once lived in seclusion on the top floor of The Mansion, hiding from the horrors of memory, revolution, and failure, many, many years ago. In 1927, he arrived in Manhattan in a long coat, and with a lowered head, his hat's brim turned down to cast his face in shadow, as if someone might recognize him and shout out his name across Times Square above the bustle of nameless masses—*hey, you there, Alexander Fyodorovich! Do you think it's so easy? You! Come back here!*—and he gripped the handle of a wicker suitcase that was still swollen with the few possessions he had gathered in haste in Paris, his former retreat. In Paris, land of the exiled, he had grown a beard, become decadent, and pushed himself beyond his fatal moderacy to cloak himself in volume and extravagance. But Kerensky could not exile Kerensky from himself. And so, he had bundled into his suitcase his half-dozen sweat-stained shirts, a portfolio of papers and letters, woolen trousers and a pair of linen, three photographs (a lost wife, a beloved dog, a demolished street), and a dozen dog-eared books with indecipherable notes scribbled in the margins of each page (his intellectual late-night musings, his undelivered speeches and other revolutions of his brandy-sodden mind). He carried a cigarette case, empty of course, and a rolled sketch of the Winter Palace in fall under a charcoal sky, smudged somewhat aggressively by the thumb of an artist who was, finally, shot in the head on a narrow street beside the Neva. Kerensky also kept folded in his left coat pocket an unexpected invitation, which offered a room, privacy, meals, rest, and endless hours of solitude in an Upper East Side residence, to dream, to forget, to revise himself. It would cost him little to nestle into the upper rooms of The Mansion, the Manhattan home of the couple Mr. and Mrs. Simpson, and to purchase his obscurity or peace.

IN 1970, Mrs. Simpson's granddaughter Cynthia and I became best friends at the Brearley School on the city's Upper East Side, where even the fourth-graders are considered exceptional young ladies gathered to blossom in bright rooms overlooking the East River. The school authorities had labeled me, like Cynthia, "a difficult child." Exceptionally difficult: moody, uncommunicative, prone to hiding under desks, or to bouts of tears, or to running away through the lobby of the school and out the gold-and-glass doors toward fresher air beside the river. Once, Cynthia threw her desk at another student, and afterward, while the teachers searched the halls for us, I hid with Cynthia in a stall in the bathroom, the lights off, for the rest of the day. We spent long hours after school at each other's small apartments where—for fun—we imitated our wealthier classmates. We imagined that chauffeurs drove us to Carl Schurz Park to play, and that on weekends, when uniforms were not required, we wore glamorous fur jackets like Tessa, Sidney, Missy, Martine, Kristina, Alissa, Sasha, and the others.

Cynthia's mother and my own mother came for the two of us after school in shabby coats, their hair blown every which way by the fall wind. They leaned awkwardly up against the Brearley's lobby wall, apart from the waiting drivers and the more elegant mothers who gathered and tapped the shoes of their high-heeled shoes impatiently, their faces exquisite and their hair coiffed. Sometimes our two mothers talked to each other, although they weren't friends. Rather, they seemed drawn to each other against their own wills and they chatted almost angrily together, as though each saw more of themselves in the other than they had ever hoped to see. My mother was a secretary, and did not earn enough money. She tried hard to avoid the subject of money, but really, there was no avoiding it when I announced that my class would be taking a trip to Russia to study history and monarchs and buildings and things. The atmosphere went gloomy. I was a scholarship student at the Brearley School, and I would not—no, I would certainly not!—be going to Russia.

"*Russia!*" my mother said, and laughed. "Are they joking? What happened to camping trips on Bear Mountain? Canoeing in the Adirondacks? A day trip to the Central Park Zoo? Why can't you study the buildings on your block like a normal kid? There are so many *flakes* over at that school!"

Only Cynthia understood. She wouldn't be going to Russia either. Instead, we would be hanging out in Cynthia's bedroom, listening to *Sergeant Pepper's Lonely Hearts Club Band* and creating fantasies of our future fortunes. "My grandmother is rich," Cynthia confided in me. "She lives in a mansion. Would you like to go there with me sometime?"

I would. And if our mothers would not let us go with our class, they must at least allow us a visit to The Mansion, right there on the city's East Side. Maybe our mothers arranged it, coolly, together in the lobby of the school. Maybe they spoke longingly about Bear Mountain, or about the Adirondacks, or about what to do with their exceptionally difficult children while everyone else under the age of twelve went off to Russia. Or maybe they wondered where two still attractive though frazzled young women might get a drink and practice their charm, and forget their troubles, and forget what they feared it would all one day come to, this work and frustration, and forget the cost of this exclusive New York City education for girls, and forget the despair they saw in each other's eyes. Who knows what they spoke of then? But at 3:15 when Cynthia and I crossed the lobby to meet our mothers, mine looked deeply relieved and Cynthia's began to rummage through her handbag with obvious annoyance at whatever was lost.

"Thank goodness you showed up," my mother said to me later as we walked home on the boardwalk beside the river. "*That* woman is a *flake*."

KERENSKY, WE HEARD, had always been friends with the beautiful widow, Mrs. Simpson. She guarded his privacy loyally, allowing no one to intrude on his meals, his studies, or his morning and evening appearances in the library of The Mansion, where he read his trashy romance novels, sniggered, and snorted to himself over racy passages he loved and twirled the fringe of a frivolous lampshade. The Mansion was filled with guests and several other boarders as well, all of them transient types privileged with some funds or some other resources, but all of them more forthcoming, of course, than Kerensky. Boarders socialized and toured the city together, but Kerensky remained in solitude and devoted himself to his writings, his revisions of unpublished articles in Russian, and his watercolors. His rooms were strewn with finished and unfinished chapters of his imaginary memoir and with his canvases of incomplete paintings of—imagine!—little kittens and bubbling brooks and holiday picnics, pastoral scenes he longed for in his shuttered rooms although his head was filled—no one knew this for a fact but Kerensky— with other, darker visions. How could he paint what he saw or what he had seen? The streets behind the palace swarmed with fools. Nevsky Prospect was littered with bodies. Grieving families clung to him, pulled at his arms, pursued him, and demanded apology. The lights of the Winter Palace were extinguished and he could hear betrayers and murderers sliding on their bellies across the Malachite Hall, rolling back the rugs, hunting him down.

He would gather up a little case of paints, pull his hat's brim low, and hurry from The Mansion just before dawn as the city started up its reassuring hum and the beautiful, irrelevant crowds swarmed around him. He would head to the East River, up toward Gracie Mansion (the city mayor's humble government), and find his favorite bench, beside which he would set up his easel and paints. He painted the dull, gray currents of an ordinary American river into which no one else he knew had looked for relief or memory, and he could feel his own blood flowing backward, toward home, toward the Neva, still flowing beneath the ice of his last provisional day.

IN MY MEMORY, The Mansion is unearthly, suspended in a visible dust that held its rooms outside of time. And the rooms I came to know well each had a distinct voice. Some voices were dark murmurs that persisted in my ear, as with the downstairs parlor, its velvet curtain drawn. Other rooms, like the vast green-carpeted Music Gallery, wailed in thin siren pitches that were unnerving, as though a soprano could not release her highest note but held it through the century as guests departed and there was no one left to listen. The dining room—all locked arched windows, surrounding a glass banquet table fit for thirty diners, but with a setting for one that faced the view of a garden of stones—sounded to me like a stifled yawn. Walking from room to room, I had the eerie feeling that the voices I was hearing, these whispers and wails and exhalations, were the voices of vanished boarders, guests, devotees who lingered on in the rooms even after their deaths. There was so much volume in such an empty place. The Mansion was surely haunted. Every creak and groan of the old elevator, rising from floor to desolate floor, signaled a ghostly presence. Who would be in the elevator, going to the fifth floor of locked suites and boxed memorabilia? Who would be descending to the basement to study the wines, or to admire the cans of fruits and pickles and sauces? Who was playing the piano in the gallery after dinner when Mrs. Simpson had retired to her rooms and the servants, Hank and An-mei, were bustling about in the kitchen? Somebody, or a whole host of phantoms, exercised their rights and claimed their domain.

Cynthia helped me sometimes to climb into The Mansion's dumbwaiter, and she would pull the cord that sent me from floor to floor, to listen and spy. I was a terrible spy and discovered nothing. Once, the dumbwaiter got stuck between floors, and I hung suspended in darkness, determined not to cry out to the ghosts to release me. An-mei, pear-shaped and gray-haired, with apologetic eyes, finally brought me back to the light of the kitchen, where she scolded us gently for our mischief. But we persisted in our investigations. We scaled the crumbling stone fountain. We peered over the wall into another barren garden. We hid in a hundred different corners of The Mansion, tried them all. Cynthia's favorite spot to hide was under the piano in the Music Gallery—the white piano, near the window. We were both too frightened to approach the black grand piano at the opposite end of the room, but we waited patiently, solemnly, for an explosion of Bach, or Mozart, to mysteriously seize its keys. Sometimes, we heard a television in the study on the second floor, and pressed our ears against the oak door. We recognized a familiar theme song playing on the set inside.

What was the ghost watching?

"*The Brady Bunch!*" Cynthia whispered.

We nodded in amazement.

"Who watches the TV upstairs?" Cynthia asked An-mei one afternoon at The Mansion as we lounged in the dirty laundry piled up in Hank and An-mei's quarters behind the kitchen. Unlike the rest of the rooms in The Mansion, these quarters were steamy, comfortable, littered with belongings and books and stacks of paper and magazines. Mobiles hung from the overhead light bulbs, lampshades tilted at angles convenient for reading, pillows were scattered all over the place—in chairs, on sofas, on the floor—and all the furniture was covered with ragged bedspreads and worn tapestries. An-mei worked at an ironing board she kept stationed in the center of the largest room, and she looked up, shaking her head.

"Who lives on the fifth floor then?" Cynthia demanded.

An-mei folded a sleeve, steamed it.

"Tell us the truth, An-mei!"

She shrugged.

"Who plays the piano then?"

An-mei beamed. "Betty plays piano! Betty is gonna be famous."

Betty was the teenage daughter of An-mei and Hank. She was a long-haired beauty who we heard studied piano at a prestigious city music school—the Juilliard School, maybe, or Diller-Quaile. She would flounce in on some afternoons, throw down her schoolbooks and her sheet music, shove crackers into her mouth, spit crumbs, and curse, "Goddamn homework!"

"So messy!" An-mei scolded her. "So rude!"

"I'm an American teenager," Betty snapped, tossing her hair. "Defiant behavior is natural."

Betty had been born after An-mei and Hank moved from China to America and she had lived in The Mansion her whole life, wandering restlessly back and forth between the maze of elegant rooms that were one realm, and the toasty cramped rooms behind the kitchen. I think An-mei and Hank tried to rein Betty in, to keep her from appearing too often in the outer halls as though she owned them, but Betty was incapable of meekness. As a child, she announced, she had purposely spilled all her marbles on the marble floor of the Grand Parlor and screamed with delight as they rolled every which way, invading the corners, scattering themselves brightly until An-mei ran after them—sixty-five loose marbles—and put them back in their place in a bucket once used for soapy water to scrub the floors. An-mei shooed toddler Betty out of sight and locked her in the pantry. At seventeen, Betty seemed to think very poorly of both her parents—"those poor blind mice" she called them— and sometimes she would imitate An-mei, cast her glance toward the floor with lowered head, round her shoulders and take small, mincing steps in circles. She also thought poorly of "the mindless aristocrat," and of just about everyone and everything related to The Mansion. Betty read thick books she carried home from the public library; she despised order and disorder equally, which kept her in constant motion, rearranging objects and furniture and thoughts. She paced around Cynthia and me, sometimes trying to recruit us to more mischief with her charm, sometimes lecturing us angrily on our complicity in "this oppressive regime." She demanded to know whose side we were on, what sort of food we preferred, what our goals were for the future, what function we thought art and politics should play in the domestic routines of a household, what tasks we were willing to attend to for ourselves and what tasks we expected others to attend to for us, and if we believed elitism was the result of education, wealth, influence, or the conspiracy of all three.

What could we say? Cynthia and I just wanted to collect paper clips from Hank's pocket, eat grape Kool Pops, and maybe get a glimpse of The Mansion's ghost. Aside from her beauty, Betty made no sense to us at all. Even music seemed, in her hands, a potent weapon. There was a small upright piano shoved up against a wall opposite the ironing board and there, Betty raged. Her hands moved furiously over the keys. Sometimes she slammed the lid after the crescendo of music, and the piano would shake with a discord of its own.

"Do you play the pianos in the Music Gallery?" Cynthia asked Betty.

"Are you kidding? Those pianos are just open caskets. Didn't you see all the dead music inside?"

According to Betty, souls were lost and loose as marbles in The Mansion. And we knew they conjured tricks, paced the upper floors, competed with human restlessness, watched *The Brady Bunch,* and set the cold pianos on fire with their ghostly sonatas.

WHEN DINNER WAS SERVED on Fridays at The Mansion, daisies floated on the surface of the water in blue china bowls at each place, silver rings engraved with "S" held the embroidered cloth napkins, eight flames swayed in lit candelabra at the table's center, and wide, gleaming platters of food were rolled in on carts by An-mei in her apron. Mrs. Simpson, close to a hundred I was sure, was rolled into the dining room seated in her wheelchair by Hank. "How do you, how do you do, children!" Mrs. Simpson screeched, tapping on her hearing aid, and then holding out a gnarled hand for us to kiss before we took our places. She kept her hair piled high in a beehive. Cynthia, educated in the manners of The Mansion, curtsied elegantly, mouthing, "Good evening, Grand-mère!"

and then she introduced me, mouthing my first, middle, and last name without sound, and I, too, curtsied, less elegantly, and we stood side by side while Mrs. Simpson inspected the tidiness of our school uniforms, our hair, and the laces of our oxfords. She cautioned us vehemently to keep our knee socks raised above the knee.

"I don't want any Oonas running around the place," she said, concerned that Oona O'Neill Chaplin had been enrolled at the Brearley School in 1941 before running off with Charlie. "Thirty-six years her senior! Appalling! I won't have it!" Mrs. Simpson cried. She directed Hank to keep an eye out for us, and Hank, from behind her wheelchair, answered loudly, "Yes, Mrs. Simpson," and never once said more than that in the year I shared the rituals of The Mansion. Hank seemed in private conversation only with himself, or with the elegant rooms, and in perpetual disagreement with the furniture, the rugs, and the lamps. He was never pleased, never flustered, and never anything but silent and thorough. Caught unaware as he was checking the dining table or composing an agenda in his notebook, his eyes would flash briefly, his intelligence bubbling up to his cracked lips, but he would adjust his coat hem and shrug his words away.

"The insides of Grand-mère's ears are blue," Cynthia said as we sat down at the table. "Be sure to look when you can."

Mrs. Simpson presided at one end of the table, facing the long expanse of empty places. Cynthia sat at her right side, and I to her left, both of us balanced on embroidered pillows An-mei had slipped onto our chairs before the bell summoned us to dine. Children were not permitted to speak except when spoken to, and even then, our comments had to be written down on small pads of paper beside our place setting and passed over to Mrs. Simpson, who did not read lips but would read our notes out loud with drama and delight. "'Yes, I do like carrots, Grand-mère.' Good! Good!" She folded the little note and put it aside. "And what about school, girls? Do you like school?"

Cynthia would look at me, nod, and it was my turn to take up a pencil and scribble back and pass my note, while she got in a few bites of food. "'School is fine. Math is hard.' Oh dear, math is hard!" The dinner went on in this way, with Cynthia and me eating between notes, and a small stack of papers accumulating beside Mrs. Simpson's finger bowl. An-mei showed us no signs of affection or interest as she carried each platter to us, then stood waiting on our left while we helped ourselves to potatoes, creamed meats, piping vegetables in sauce. I remember looking up at her once, helplessly, while I pursued with a spoon the last of the potatoes that rolled around the enormous platter she held for me, but she kept her eyes downcast, even when I picked the potato up with my hand and placed it as elegantly as possible onto my plate. I glanced over at Hank, who stayed beside the wall, his hands folded behind him, and I hoped that I saw assurance in his gaze. Dinner was a lonely, tiring event that demanded complete concentration as well as skill at selecting the proper fork, cleansing appropriately between courses, and remaining composed in the presence of so many beautiful plates. I thought, sometimes, of my mother as I had discovered her one afternoon in our little kitchen at home, shattering one plate after another on the squares of our linoleum floor, and sobbing. "What are you doing to all our plates, Mom?" I had asked cautiously and she had paused briefly in her work to cry, "*I broke my heirloom crystal bowl! It should have been all of these! These are nothing!*" She resumed her smashing until there was nothing left.

I wished she could see all of the crystal at The Mansion.

One evening, someone else besides Mrs. Simpson sat with us at The Mansion's dinner table—an old, boisterous priest who ate his food vigorously and wiped his mouth several times between each mouthful of food. He passed more notes to Mrs. Simpson than I could have written in an afternoon, and he told jokes to Cynthia, nudged her repeatedly with an elbow. He wanted to know what we girls did around The Mansion, how we entertained ourselves.

"We play," Cynthia said, giving him a condescending stare. She hated jokes and idle conversation.

"Ah!" He clapped his hands and gasped. "Play! Yes! The interactive possibilities are limitless! We are social creatures, aren't we? Always in pursuit of our pleasure principle, our own expressive system of survival! I envy you girls. I myself no longer play, except of course in the dispensing of spiritual advice." He winked and nudged Cynthia, who glared. We found all his talk hard to follow, especially his conversation with Mrs. Simpson, as it was part written, part spoken, part screeched, but it was the priest, I believe, who first mentioned Kerensky's name.

"I do miss that communal atmosphere, that is to say, *seeing* others," he said, "but times change, they must, and so must the social contracts. Perhaps that's best. But it was a comfort back then to know so many boarders and guests, to hear the sounds of company, even from the quiet ones, in my view. The foreigners were so polite, weren't they? The Czech? Those sweet Danish sisters? Am I the only one left living? I think I am! A remarkable feat! Should we consider Donavetsky? He keeps to himself, shy soul. And my God—forgive me!—but Kerensky! Notorious fellow. I admit he might have had a certain vigor in his youth, a certain inevitable foreign maverick appeal, for ladies, that is," the old priest concluded, wiping his mouth, then coughing. "But I suppose he had good cause to keep quiet when he pleased, didn't he? He surely did."

"What?" Mrs. Simpson shouted.

The priest reached for his notepad and began to scribble his words.

"KERENSKY WAS A RUSSIAN KING, or maybe some sort of general. He was very handsome and powerful. He lived in a huge Winter Palace that all the people admired, until one winter it fell down—probably because there was so much snow—it just collapsed! And then there was a revolution or a war and everyone in the land was murdered. Then Kerensky wandered all over the world looking for some place to live, and then he came here and fell in love with my grandmother. I think that's what happened."

"Did he die here in The Mansion?" I asked Cynthia, the keeper of secrets.

She nodded wisely. "He must've. Or else—" she breathed, "He's still here!"

We determined to find Alexander Kerensky.

That evening the elevator popped and whirred as Cynthia pushed the heavy handle and took us up through the many stories of The Mansion to the fifth floor. There were no lights, no windows, the doors to all four suites of rooms—locked—faced one another across the elegant hall, blankly. We tiptoed toward a particularly ornate door on the left, then knelt and pressed our faces against the floor so we might peer underneath. Death, we assumed, was everywhere—leaning up against us in the stillness, breathing down our collars, scurrying with a wayward ball of dust toward our open mouths. There was a cough. A chair scraped. We heard a footstep, a distinctly foreign footstep! We leapt to our feet and pounded on the button for the elevator that had departed, leaving us alone with the dead. Panicked, Cynthia yanked at a door that led to the servants' stairwell, and we raced down the five flights and then a sixth, toward the cheerful yellow rooms of the canning cellar, and it was there that we discovered the paintings we knew must be Kerensky's, his paintings of the Horses of the Revolution.

The horses pranced on the walls in fabulous, glorious watercolors, one horse beside every step, rearing, snorting, and pawing the invisible earth, galloping toward some unknown victory or battle. Cynthia breathed loudly, my heart fluttered away in my chest, but we were silent and in awe as we studied the paintings we had stumbled on in our fear. Who had stood there, brush in hand in the cellar alone, day after day, painting these fierce animals? We exchanged a glance. Some of the horses had riders, wild-eyed men in black fur and tall hats, with moustaches curling up as they yanked on the reins of their stallions. The walls were alive. Surely this was Kerensky's lonely frenzy of art hidden in a canning cellar.

My mother came for me at The Mansion after dark. I remember that she seemed always reluctant to set foot in The Mansion, although she never forbade me going there. I could not understand her reticence. Wasn't The Mansion so much better than our own tiny apartment, a fourth-floor walk-up, with peeling paint and bars on all the windows? Wasn't it a relief to move through the wide spaces of The Mansion and to know that if you got bored of one room, you could choose from fifty others? Wasn't it wonderful to have meals served to you and to have a gold elevator carry you whenever you were tired, and to have bells in every room, to summon company or help? After the doorbell rang announcing through the halls my mother's arrival, Cynthia and I would sit together on the marble steps in the front foyer and watch my mother pace back and forth between the glass doors and the front gate. She must have noticed us there, watching her, not running to greet her, but she pretended not to notice. She was polite to An-mei, who opened the doors, but she would never step across the threshold onto the polished floor. "Are you ready to leave?" she asked me routinely, and I'd say "No," and Cynthia would put in a good word for me, suggesting that I be allowed to stay just a little longer. My mother's thin mouth told me I wouldn't be staying and that she only tolerated Cynthia in my life because we were exceptionally difficult children and needed her tolerance.

"Have you said your goodbye to Mrs. Simpson? And thanked her?" Why did my mother look so wrong, so awkward standing there, so very out of place? She seemed to have come from a completely different world, which of course she had and she knew it, and she drew the line clearly, and literally, between herself and those things she knew she would never have. I sensed then that there were things that I *could* have, places I could go that my mother could not, and the knowledge made me feel powerful and embarrassed for us both and eager to flaunt my wealth of possibility in her face. She kept her hands in her pockets; she stomped snow impatiently from her boots onto the welcome mat; she thanked An-mei for all her trouble and asked, "How is your daughter, An-mei?" To which An-mei would reply, blushing, "She's a good girl," and my mother's glad nod to An-mei seemed to incriminate me as she pushed her own child out the door into the winter and bracing air of another world. Her world.

"The Mansion is haunted, Mother."

"Mm?"

"There's a ghost. From Russia," I told her. My remark received only silence until she said, "*We're going home*" and took my hand, not looking at me at all.

KERENSKY DID NOT haunt The Mansion, but us. He followed us through the rooms. He whispered in our ears all the secrets that bore us through our ordinary days. Cynthia and I were his only contacts in the visible world, we believed, which is why Alexander Fyodorovich Kerensky's actual appearance in the flesh on a cold, quiet day in winter, was so unexpected. We might have imagined him, but I think we did not. A terrible scene had erupted shortly before we discovered him, so we assumed he had manifested because he was stirred by all the music and the shouting. Perhaps he was bothered, as we knew spirits often are, by too much noise. Or, more likely, Kerensky wanted to watch us.

Cynthia and I knelt on the floor of the Grand Parlor. We could hear Betty shrieking in the back rooms, as if she had, indeed, seen a ghost. Then she banged wildly on the keys of her piano, creating a terrific, violent dirge. And we could hear that An-mei was crying, pleading unintelligible words to her daughter beneath the torrent of music. Betty slammed shut the lid of the piano. She screamed, "I hate this awful place! You can't tell me I'm not going! It's my first tour! You just want to keep me here because you're afraid I won't come back! You're afraid of the whole world! You're afraid of me! You want me to die without seeing anything! I'd rather die than live like this, like a parasite. Why can't you get it? Things have changed!"

Cynthia and I stood up as Betty moved past us, finally a loose marble herself, unseeing, her bulging book bag slung over her shoulder as though in it were all her most beloved possessions gathered for her final exit. An-mei scurried along behind her daughter, wringing a dish towel in her hands and still weeping for her good girl, her Betty. We had never seen An-mei like this, so undone, so bereft. The scene was unbearable to watch. Betty let the iron gate slam shut in An-mei's face, and An-mei was left alone, everything changed. Cynthia and I slipped quietly up the stairs and out of sight, mortified.

Then, as we continued our ascent, we heard over An-mei's sobs and diminishing footsteps, the mutterings of the television. The doors to the second-floor study stood wide open. And there he was. Or, there *someone* was, an old man, slumped over in an armchair. He dozed, then lifted his head, then dozed once more. Kerensky? Kerensky!

"Oh, come in, children! Little ones!" Kerensky snorted to life. He wore old leather bedroom slippers and gray woolen socks that were gathered around his ankles, and he held a tattered cardigan tightly around himself. He smiled, but he was seemingly half-blind and unable to focus precisely on us. His teeth were yellow and pointed at various angles inside his mouth, and his hair hung in a wayward lock across his cheek. His gestures were quick and approachable, like a child's, and he pointed to the rug and said in a thick and halting English, "Have a seat, this is a good show of television, I think you must like it," so we entered the study and sat beside him.

Our new friend was all alone, he confided to us sadly, and disliked by his grown children—two boys, one an architect, the other a literary man—who had apartments of their own that they did not allow him to enter. He had no place to go; he kept to himself. He had no friends except for Mrs. Simpson, who had taken him in some time ago, and he stayed on, finding solace only in his music, his drawings, his memoirs (several volumes, he anticipated, which took almost all of the energy that he had left), and in letters to friends who were no longer living but lived in his mind's eye in the homeland from which he had exiled himself so many years before. Perhaps we two children would now become his friends? How he longed for a decent conversation! He liked chocolate, *General Hospital,* his walks beside the East River on brisk fall days, though not so much in winter, which brought him pain in his heart and knees, and he liked also backgammon. Did we know backgammon? We did not, but he taught us slowly, kindly, and for hours that afternoon the three of us played tournaments of backgammon, laughing, claiming victories, shaking hands, and never speaking of the past, or of revolutions, or of the extinguished Winter Palace we knew had once been the home of all his power and greatness. There was no need to speak of that, or to remind our friend of his old sorrows. He giggled with us until dusk.

"How was it," Cynthia asked him bravely, "where you used to live?"

"Very cold," he said and we knew not to ask him anything else.

We told no one, not even An-mei or Hank, of our new and secret alliance. We had made promises, we had made plans. We had agreed to meet Kerensky whenever we could so that he might instruct us in more elaborate strategies for backgammon. When he fell asleep smiling in his armchair as though he was pleased to have taught us so well, we had even kissed his chapped face, lovingly. Certainly, we never thought that on the whim that belongs only to those who have already departed, Kerensky would suddenly vanish—as would Betty, and An-mei, and Hank, and even, one day, my mother—without a word goodbye.

ALEXANDER FYODOROVICH KERENSKY, I have read, arrived in Manhattan on a dark and bitter day of winter, February 3rd, 1927, ten years after the end of the Revolution, his torn ticket for the SS *Olympic* crumpled in his pocket and his breath quick as his ship approached New York Harbor. He was still a young man. Jostled along in the arriving crowds, tripping once on the steep walkway that stretched toward foreign land, he searched the waiting faces and hoped for one friend, one ally onshore. He could speak no English. He was scheduled to give a lecture—but what could he say?—to the New York community gathered at the Century Theater, and he feared how he might be translated and received. With cheers? Hisses? He spotted the faces of those who would become his friends in those exiled years and also later, when he returned to Manhattan an old blind man in his eighties. There was Vinner, a bespectacled professor of Russian at Columbia University and Vinner's broad wife, Ludmila; and the Strunskys, a couple of gregarious journalists; and, I have read, Kerensky saw one Kenneth F. Simpson, an assistant U.S. attorney, who stood holding the hand of a tall and beautiful woman, Simpson's soon-to-be-widowed wife.

That is a very different story, made of someone else's fictions and facts—a story I learned only when The Mansion had sunk into my past. But The Mansion is hardly less vivid to me now than on what I believe was the last evening I saw it and saw the world I believed would be mine. My mother had come for me, as usual, but perhaps she was suffering a little bit more than usual. The New York winter was long, her burden of financial responsibility was heavy, and she had taken another job that year as a receptionist, working late hours. She was beaten, tired, and in no mood for a difficult child, or to stand anymore on the line between what she had and what she did not. Inspired, maybe, by her defeated look, I resisted her eagerness to get my coat and to force me from The Mansion I loved. I stood with my shoulder against Cynthia's and my feet firmly planted. I refused to go. "I'm not going with you," I told my

mother. I had An-mei, Hank, Cynthia, and a new addition to my family
of cherished exiles, Kerensky. I did not speak his name. His name was
in my blood. I was ready to claim my new life.

We battled it out in the foyer of The Mansion. My mother wrenched
my hand out of Cynthia's. I started screaming, *"No!"* She shoved my
arms through the sleeves of my coat and when I screamed louder, she
shook me back and forth. "It's time to go and that's the end of it." I
twisted and tried to squirm out of my coat and when I couldn't free
myself, I cried, "I don't want to go! I want to stay here forever! I hate it
at home! I hate you! You're hurting me!" My mother stepped away from
me and gazed at me, her face suddenly blank. She didn't need to hold
me to own me, that much was clear to me then. "Can you hear me?" she
said. *"This is the end."*

I gave a glance to Cynthia, and to An-mei, who turned away from me,
or from all daughters, and with my mother I exited The Mansion and the
gate closed permanently behind us.

I HAVE LOOKED for The Mansion a few times when I have been back
in Manhattan for work or errands. The buildings in that part of town
look plain and blank and undistinguished to me. Every gate looks both
familiar and wrong—close, but not the iron gate I think I am looking for.
Cynthia became a therapist somewhere in the Northwest, I have heard.
Mrs. Simpson has long been dead. Her obituary ran in the city papers in
the early 1980s I believe, alongside a picture of her in her youth, with a
wide and generous smile. An-mei's death and Hank's I can only imagine,
An-mei nodding off as she rested beside a pile of laundry and failing to
wake, and years later, Hank clutching his chest in the canning cellar
and covering his mouth to stifle his own cry. I imagine Betty too—that
she heard about her parents' deaths from Toronto, or from Paris, or
London, or maybe from just across town where she lived in a one-room
apartment with two cats and an upright piano she never played. And

the lonely foreign tenant I knew only as my friend, the ghost Alexander Fyodorovich Kerensky, one day departed The Mansion and was taken in by a forgiving son, the architect.

I would not have believed any of this as my mother and I marched away from what we both longed for, leaving our footprints in the snow. I looked around at the white world. *So many flakes.* I thought I was hearing Betty play a wild, dramatic music, the music of tirade and escape, and I saw, in my mind's eye, Kerensky's Winter Palace, its hundred spires reflecting back the moon and then toppling, pitching downward to the earth. The windows shattered, a storm of glass fell on the square, and the stones crumbled, slowly at first, and then each stone crushed the other stones beneath it and everything cascaded in dust and quaking slabs, sending up white waves of snow. The Neva River overflowed its shores, and our palace was covered by darkness.

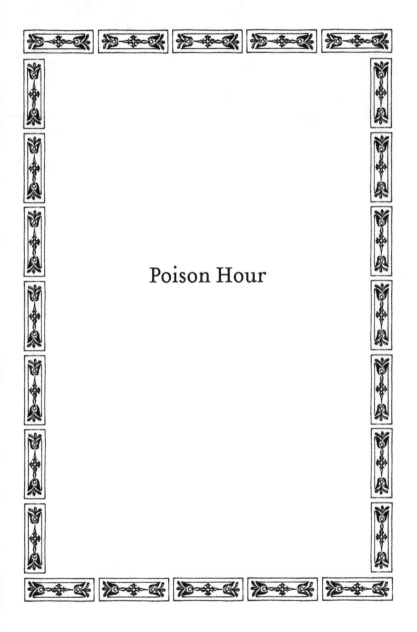

Poison Hour

E VERY AFTERNOON, trucks cruised the neighborhood spraying poison. My mother kept the children—my sister, my two cousins, and me—locked indoors for at least an hour before and after the poison descended, to protect us from seizures, cancer, asphyxiation, and death. The poison was meant to kill mosquitoes, but it did not. It did kill the large rabbit we kept in a cage at the end of the lawn, because *"you must never let a rabbit out of its cage or it will be killed."* I sat in my room during the poison hours, the room I called the Dead Bug Room, suffocating weirdly big, blood-stuffed mosquitoes under an empty candy jar while my sister read Nancy Drew novels. She loved the way Nancy solved all the mysteries. And my cousins, visiting for a couple of months, were some-where down a long, humid hallway, making Play-Doh jewelry they pasted onto their ears, and hung around their throats, and later, when vampires arrived to suck our blood, garlic threaded on string. That was my idea.

Many things that summer had a formal name: our summer rental house was the House on Hodge Road. Then there was the Dead Bug Room, the Good Bathroom, and the Nasty Bathroom, which had no window and a blue metal sliding door that was badly rusted. The large living room was the Theatre, which had freestanding bookshelves that could serve as wings, a hidden entrance behind a fake wall, a polished floor, and track lighting. We would put on a show! That was my sister's idea. We would charge a dollar per construction paper ticket and invite all the parents we could think of to be our audience. Mr. Bailey's tree, with muscled, graceful limbs that stretched over to our side of the Big Hedge, was the Absolutely Lethal Tree—*that tree could be absolutely lethal,* my mother often said. The car, my father's old station wagon, which chugged home each morning around 3:00 a.m. when his gigs were over and a natural nighttime mist had settled over the suburbs, was the Maid of the Mist. I was always wide awake to hear the Maid of the Mist pull into the driveway and sputter out, sounding as though she would never start again.

My father was home.

I heard the sound of his sax case clunk down on the step, then the rattle of the door, the jingle of keys, his heavy sighs and raps on the glass. I stared at the ceiling and scratched my mild mosquito bites—at night they felt almost good, really—and my sister snored heavily and sometimes slapped herself in her sleep when mosquitoes landed on her arms. The mosquitoes wanted my sister, they seemed to lust for her blood most of all. She looked increasingly pale and anemic through the hot months as her enthusiasm for play was sucked steadily out of her. Her limbs began to swell and pucker in one red scabrous rash, and before the summer ended, she would be sequestered all day in the air-conditioned master bedroom, ice packs pressed against her body as she watched episodes of *Get Smart* and *I Spy*. She watched my daily mosquito suffocation rituals with skepticism. "It's no use," she said. "You can't fight them." I understood only that my sister had the right blood and I did not. "Your sister's blood," my mother explained, "is close to the surface of her skin." Low-flying suckers could detect its heat. But they could not detect the heat of my blood, and, undernourished, they gave up and moved on.

How long would my father wait outside the door for my mother to let him in? Her job was to hurry downstairs, unlock the door, and let my father enter. She kept the door locked when he was gone because, "It's a strange house," she said darkly, meaning, I think, *It's not our house,* or possibly, *We don't have a house, only a small city apartment and so we are uneasy in this large rental house that might seem small to* some *people but which to us is unmanageable, intimidating, haunted,* a house to which my father seemed never to have the right key, although my father possessed many keys he kept in his pockets with his loose change. The keys required a special chain. There was a black leather case for extra keys too, yet my father never had the right key at the right time. He tried many different keys and he rarely located the right one. Sometimes he could even *hear* the keys, but not find them. They were lost in the cuff of his trousers or in the hem of his jacket while he retraced his steps looking for them. He was many times left baffled and stranded on the wrong side of doors. "Don't you have your keys?" my mother, the doorkeeper, always asked my father once the door was open.

"Yes, I have my keys," he would answer and step across the threshold. They would go to bed with the matter settled between them—the matter, that is, of the uselessness of all keys and of my father having keys at all; the matter of his always needing to be let in—needing to *ask* to be let in—and of my mother determining whether or not he would be.

My mother was thirty-six then, very slim, with dark hair she kept curled with pointed metal clips and wire rollers she wore in bed each night when she slept. "Of course, they hurt me," she said. "But that is the price you must pay for beauty." She had healthy, freckled skin. She wore no makeup. She liked to wear red bandanas, tight orange stretch-pants and cotton T-shirts, or green-and-white-striped sundresses, with jade earrings in her ears. She looked fabulous. "May I have your earrings when you die?" I asked my mother once, and she replied sadly, "I suppose so. Is that all you want?" In a photo taken that summer—I think I took the photo myself, learning to use my mother's Kodak Instamatic—she sits beside my father, holds his hand, smiling, and they both appear happy, but neither one of them looks at the camera. They look in opposite directions and down, as though something approaches them through the grass, on either side. My mother appears so young in this picture I cannot square the image with my memory of her frail in a hospital gown, at the end of her life, or even with the way she appeared to me that summer—as a swift power in her white *see-through* negligee patrolling the long halls and unused rooms of the House on Hodge Road at night.

I didn't know then that my mother had hoped for several years after she married my father and even after they had children, that she would become a popular movie actress or a celebrity—someone bathed in love and attention; or that she had liked to act and dance, and that she had a gift for dance, in particular, the sort of natural fire and exuberance that draws looks, admiration, and desire. My mother and father had met one night in college when she went to a dance and fell in love with the swing music she was dancing to, and told the sax player in the band, my father, that he was great, incredibly talented. I did not know that before that dance, my father had served in the Second World War for two years in the Special Services Entertainment Corps—he did not fight, he played— and even when I came to know this, I didn't understand it. I imagined my father, silhouetted on the battlefield, earth exploding around him while he played a sad tune and soldiers closed their eyes and died in heaps around him. In these fantasies, he wore a crisp uniform and his hat tipped at a jaunty angle. Years later, I thought I learned how it *really* was: the worn-out musicians piled onto trucks that drove them, in the end, through liberated camps that stank of flesh and death. My father mentioned these army trucks, every now and then, and the trucks were all I knew about his war, or about the "Great War," as he called it, which he said is what you must call *any* war that you are *in*. The trucks traveled in single file, and once, when he was ordered to do so, he leapt from the top of one of these trucks and damaged his feet, which might explain the limp that made him lurch through life like a drinker, although he never was one. I pictured the musicians—the drummers, the bass players, the keyboard guys, the horn players like my dad—all leaping from these trucks into those camps my sister had told me about. Maybe the musicians looked for souvenirs of war, something prisoners had left behind: small figurines of stoic, Aryan-looking men of porcelain and wood, like the two that watched us from a top shelf of my father's library. Maybe the musicians entered the abandoned offices where commandants had left their valuable paperweights made of bullets and blades and all things the very opposite of music. Who, exactly, had taught the soldier-musicians how to play? I wondered. My father never said. I heard his music only when he played his saxophone at summer parties of drinking, dancing, and loud singing. I clung, like my sister, like a burr, to my father's arm whenever he made music.

"Is this the right key?" he would ask the crowd, and then start up a song. My mother would join in the song, her voice light and lively, until her frown. "Not the right one?" my father would say curiously, and start the song again.

I didn't know what my father did when he left the house. I did not know what it meant that he was a musician. I had no idea why my father always went off to play with the guys—faceless, unknowable men—while my sister and I played Parcheesi and checkers and badminton and Play-Doh at home. The Poison Hours were long, quiet, empty of my father, and dank with boredom.

My mother liked to read crime novels in a white leather lounge chair on the sundeck after the sun went down and the toxins had settled. She sipped a pale drink she called Tom Collins. When my mother and Tom Collins got together, there was nothing then for the four kids to do but watch horror movies—*The Picture of Dorian Gray*, *The Haunting*, *The Island of Lost Souls*, *Horror Hotel*—and eat potato chips. My sister, a cotton blanket draped over her head to keep the mosquitoes away from her neck, explained the movies seriously to me and to our cousins (Jessie nodded, but Liz was only four, too young to get anything) and with a certain flair that would take her, in her early thirties, into a theatrical career. "That's what Dorian would really look like," my sister explained, "if he hadn't bargained away his soul. He'd be ugly, like the picture. It's a story about cheating time, so you don't have to see who you really are. You stay beautiful-looking and people put up with you no matter what you do. Everything looks fine, but it isn't. Get it?" Mosquitoes settled on the potato chips in a bowl at my sister's feet, and one afternoon while the bugs swarmed around her and tears rolled down her cheeks. I sprayed Off! on all the chips and on her feet, too, which were wrapped in layers of socks.

"Why do you just sit there?" I yelled at her. "Why don't you do something?"

On the television screen, a young woman gasped and stumbled through the cemetery, and her boyfriend, not quite dead yet, staggered toward the zombies with a flaming cross balanced on his shoulders— very dramatic in black and white. My sister yelled back with startling vitality, "She sprayed the potato chips with bug spray and we're all eating them now! Is that okay, Mom?" After that, I heard my mother's voice as she talked at my father on the phone, her pitch rising quickly. My father was somewhere, playing, and my mother had that *I-can't-handle-it-where-are-you* voice I didn't know I would come to identify easily and would hear again and again through her life, and when she was dead, in my own throat.

"The children have poisoned themselves! They're all going to die! They've got to go to the hospital! All of them!"

My sister gazed at the television.

WE BEGAN REHEARSALS for our production of *Ali Baba and the Forty Thieves* in July, with plans to perform the play at the end of the month. My sister had seen a production of *Ali Baba* in New York City with her classmates, and she thought it would be good material to produce as a Broadway show in the living room when my mother suggested we do something with our lives. My mother wanted some time to relax now in the afternoon with her drinks and her book, one of the long series of paperbacks featuring a detective who had, according to the title, the girl, the gold watch, and everything! The girl pictured on the cover kneeling in front of an enormous watch was much like the girl on the cover of many of my mother's books that summer, tanned and luscious and draped in a flimsy bright gown. On the cover's corner was an image of the blank-faced detective who would discover the woman's body. My mother knew all the details.

My sister, my cousins, and I met in the stuffy room that would be our small theater. We cut out tickets, designed the program, and wrote and rewrote our stage directions—*they enter the dukedom with a clever plan* or *they enter the Cave and emerge loudly wealthy.* My sister recruited Sally and Doogie Bailey, which meant we had to walk, cautiously, under the Lethal Tree and knock on Mr. Bailey's door, and speak to Bob Bailey's freckled wife Claire, who sometimes knocked impatiently on our door too. My sister, as Casting Director, assigned Jessie the role of the Evil Duke, for no reason I could see since Jessie seemed to me to be the least evil of us, but she accepted the role with dignity. Liz would wear green pajamas with pom-poms, and cardboard floppy ears, in her own role as Little Donkey; Sally, a white nightgown as the Sliding Cave Door (a role I had wanted for myself); Doogie, a pair of shorts and a patch over his eye as the only visible and slow-witted yodeling thief.

"And you," my sister said to me, "you'll be Morjana. She's the servant."

"I don't want to be the servant."

"Don't worry. You don't have to be smart, just pretty. She saves everyone. Wear a nightgown and a hankie on your head."

She dressed herself in a baggy shirt of my mother's, orange pants, and sandals, as Ali Baba the Mastermind.

"Who's going to see this play anyway?" I demanded. "Is Dad going to see us?"

My mother encouraged us to rehearse as often as possible, every afternoon just as professionals would, and so we sweated away in the living room for weeks, made up lines as we went along and yelled at Liz, who kept falling down, tripping on her floppy donkey ears, and crying. Sally complained often that she could not keep her arms extended, as a cave door would, for the entire duration of the play. Jessie wondered what we would do without a curtain to lower when the play was over. After some debate, we agreed to indicate *the end* by lowering our heads and eyes. My sister said an audience always knows when a play is over even if the actors are all still onstage, because nothing else happens. "We just show the ways things begin. The audience has to *imagine* what the characters do next." We ate Popsicles, drew faces and outfits on the sticks when we were done, laughed a lot, and argued about the script. Does Ali Baba say, "Open Sesame" to the sealed cave door, or "Open Says Me"? Both worked for us, or else Sally couldn't tell the difference.

Mosquitoes crawled along the furniture like ants and became bright bursts of blood on the chintz when we smacked them in their tracks. Wearily, my sister adjusted her pink tortoiseshell glasses, held together with tape, and scratched her arms and legs. She peeled away bloody Band-Aids. She was tight-lipped and authoritative when we could not remember what to do or what came next. "We have to pull this together, people," she said. "Do you realize we don't have much time?" Rehearsals usually broke up when the afternoon horror flicks came on or the four of us grew bored of one another, or we simply wandered away in different directions. The air leaned hard against the windows of the house. The hiss and rumble of the trucks crescendoed up the street.

Sometimes I snuck out of the house into the poison, hardly breathing. I poked my way through the weeds beside the front door. I climbed up a water pipe onto a narrow ledge that ran just beneath the windows. The toes of my red sneakers stuck out over the ledge, but there was enough room for me to keep my balance and inch my way slowly around the entire house. I called this "orbiting." Miraculously, my mother always sensed, no matter where she was or what she was doing, when I had slipped away from her into the dangerous air. "Where is she? Where exactly is she? She didn't go outside did she? Is she here?" I heard my mother demand all this of no one in particular it seemed—no one ever answered. My sister might shrug or lift an eyebrow. My mother's calls got louder and her tone shifted from anxiety to anger and finally to panic if she heard the poison trucks arrive on the streets. *Mom, calm down, please, calm down,* I whispered to myself, and occasionally I still do, although now she is gone and buried, her panic buried inside me. Calmly, I traveled around the house and saw shapes and pictures form in the space behind each window. Through the glass, I could locate everyone inside the house, and then move on, planetary and uninvolved. On some rare days of my orbit, my father manifested unexpectedly, alone on the other side of the window. I watched him fill his glass of lemonade with too much sugar and then stir much too long, while he listened to the percussion of the spoon. Sometimes I watched him shine his shoes atop the stove, polish them with cream in a fascinating rhythm. Once, I spotted him outside reclining in a lawn chair, his dark glasses balanced on the end of his nose, a newspaper open across his lap as he slept.

There was no wonder my mother had fallen hard for him when they met. He was a handsome, if disheveled, man. In daylight, his black close-cut hair was uncombed and his face was unshaven. His loose sweater had not yet torn—it was only beginning to fray. He had three dark, gracefully arched eyebrows. His left brow was interrupted by a dramatic scar on which no hair had ever grown, not since that day when he was six years old and had chased his neighbor Audrey across the street in front of a careening truck. (This also might have been the cause of his limp.) Often, I tried to picture Audrey, her blond braid flying as she ran, and then Audrey, halted and confused on a curbside while my father lay in the street caught beneath the truck's front tire. But for some reason I always reversed the precise details of this chase, and instead saw Audrey chasing my father. Perhaps I did not want to think of my father chasing Audrey, or worse, of what made Audrey so special that he would chase her. Maybe, I wanted to hold Audrey responsible in some way for all my father's pains.

In photographs, he wore gray shiny suits with stiff shoulders, neckties perfectly tied, and his hair slicked back. He stood with his feet planted wide apart, and his sax at his lips. He kept his eyes focused downward, toward dancing feet and the hems of skirts that circled round him; toward polished floors, and flung confetti; toward streamers tangled around high-heeled shoes; or toward the lowest notes of jazz. Ashtrays spun thin threads of smoke, ice cubes rattled in glasses, tiny tables wobbled, and open, lipsticked mouths blew kisses and begged for favorite tunes, "The Party's Over" and "Smoke Gets in Your Eyes," and "Have I Stayed Too Long at the Fair?" In these photographs, he stood in front of smaller men who watched him and waited for the signal of a new tune, a big finish, a different key. My father knew the right key, every time. At home, he was tired from playing at night. At home, music hummed inside his head, background to my mother's voice, or to her occasional slammed door. Did she want to fight? He was tired from playing. He dozed. He seemed unreachable in the center of the lawn, far from our empty rabbit cage. Softly, a radio played jazzy music beside him in the grass.

When dusk came, long after my father grabbed his sax, started up the Maid of the Mist and drove away, the four of us—we forty thieves—stopped speaking. There was silence, the dank air, rain often, and the high whine of mosquitoes at our ears and at our throats. I grabbed my neck, or hit my head and ears, hoping to beat the mosquitoes back even though I knew the noisy ones are harmless. My sister had told me she read that in a book. "It's the ones you can't hear that drink your blood. Those are the females. The males make all the noise."

Why did the females want to drink blood?

"Because," my sister explained, "it's a fertility ritual. It makes them stronger."

I stared uneasily at the long halls, at the cobwebbed ceiling of my bedroom, and at the shadows on the walls of the empty guest room. I dusted each room with a rag my mother gave me. My heart pounded. I pulled stiff draperies aside to dust the windowsills, and found dead flies. I kept it to myself that I was frightened by the pale man at the window of a house in the recent Creature Feature we had watched. His face had appeared angry, desperate, as he pulled draperies aside to look for his missing bride. Clearly, he did not know that his bride was in the basement, about to have a stake driven through her heart by the town's old priest. She was very beautiful, with blonde bangs and wide eyes. But she bit people and drank their blood. Then she sobbed and ran whenever the sun came up or a cross flashed across her face. Soon, everyone she knew fell into ashes at the gates to the cemetery, although the priest had nailed garlic onto everybody's door in anticipation of this.

My sister sighed heavily when I suggested that we nail garlic to the doors and that she, my cousins, and I all wear garlic necklaces too. Nevertheless, she joined in the threading of cloves we would string round our necks. Her arms and legs were swollen and wrapped in long scarves of bandage. Her cheeks puffed up toward her eyes. She was often too miserable to direct our play, and it was my sister who finally suggested the construction paper crosses—pink, orange, green, fuchsia—Scotch-taped onto all the windows. We dressed the doors in garlic. I found it difficult to know what was really going on in a house with so many doors. I feared whatever creature might lurk behind them. In particular, I feared the rusted door of the Nasty Bathroom, which screeched as someone struggled to get into, or out of it; the master bedroom door, which my mother closed to keep the room cool, a sanctuary for my bitten sister; the study doors which my mother closed for privacy, to read the last, critical pages of her mystery; and the playroom doors, which my cousins closed when they made their secret Play-Doh jewels, or sang in unison, "Ashes! Ashes! We all fall down!" or a longer song they knew with several verses about the assorted terrible deaths of a cat, and an eerie chorus: "But the cat came back the very next day, the cat came back! They thought he was a goner! Oh, the cat came back! No, he just wouldn't go away!" My cousins and I studied the book of magic my father had given me for my birthday. I had already learned all the magic tricks to show my father and astound him. I could conceal a white Styrofoam dove inside a black sack, and then discover it, magically, in my hand, its wire claws wrapped around a golden ring. Sometimes the silence of the house was like the silence inside the sack.

AT THE FAR END of the lawn, a badminton net sagged. Every now and then, my mother gave my sister and me racquets, sunglasses, and hats, and sent us out into the morning gloom to hit the birdie. We needed some sport in our life, something more meaningful than theater. Neither of us was as accomplished at tree climbing as Jessie, who sat on a large branch at the edge of the yard and gazed over at Mr. Bailey's larger branch and swimming pool. The two branches waved to one another. My sister and I walked down the lawn and faced each other, racquets dangling, then wandered in circles for a while, until one of us said, "Okay, let's hit this thing back and forth." We could usually go for two or three volleys before the birdie bounced off her rim or mine. We trekked over to retrieve it and start over. "What a moronic game," my sister said after a while, "do people seriously spend their time doing this?"

We glanced at the house, and kept at it. Once, we perked up a bit when the screen door of the house opened, and both my mother, jersey- and slipper-clad, and my father, in khakis and old T-shirt, came out of the house together and headed down our way. "Think he's going to play with us?" I asked my sister. "Dunno," she said, and shrugged. My mother and my father both had racquets and they took sides, my father on my side of the net, and my mother with my sister. The game took off then, briefly. My mother laughed and leapt in graceful and irrelevant angles. Somehow, she always managed to hit the birdie in one lucky shot after another, and my father used his strong tennis swing to keep her running. He shouted encouraging words to my sister, who seemed to panic, or to become distressed with her bandages. My mother wanted to win and she shouted at my sister too, "Come on! Come on! You don't have to be athletic, just swing!" It seemed to me that no one was hitting the birdie my way at all. I flung my racquet in fury. I had tried a similar maneuver during a Chinese checkers tournament the previous summer, which was a bigger thrill since all the marbles went flying in colorful directions, but I found that I achieved the same overall effect in badminton—that is, *stopping the game.*

"All right, that's it," my mother said to me. She tossed her own racquet away and turned back toward the house. "You don't know how to play."

My father said, "You two kids keep playing by yourselves. I'm going to see where your Momma went."

My sister and I faced each other again. "Great," she said, "Good for you." I picked up my racquet. A white moth flew around my head, over the net and back, like a stray piece of confetti. I swung at it. The moth plummeted into the grass.

"It's just a moth!" my sister said immediately. She anticipated my next move. "You didn't do it on purpose!"

"I killed it!" I wailed.

"You kill mosquitos all the time! What's the difference?"

I turned my back on my sister and carried the moth into the house. I supposed it would probably die. That night, when I saw my sister enter the Nasty Bathroom cautiously and slide the door shut behind her to apply her pink cream and Band-Aids alone, I kept vigil beside the moth. I watched it spin in circles, and lift its wings up toward the light bulb. I heard my sister yell for help inside the bathroom. She sounded frustrated, then panicked, then afraid. She rattled the rusted door that wouldn't give, sobbed, as surely, I would have sobbed too, and pounded her palms and fists against the metal. When my mother asked me, "Where is your sister? Where is she? Do you know?" I said that I did not.

THE NOON HOUR that heralded our performance of *Ali Baba and the Forty Thieves* was bright, sunny, and rare. Sunlight drove the mosquitoes into silence; their hum beside our ears subsided. We learned that there would be no poison trucks that day, which meant the noon light could travel freely across the lawn, or toward the pool, or onto the porch and balconies, even into the house. In the hall behind the bookshelf, the Town and Country Troupe, as we had named ourselves, prepared for our audience. I slipped into my blue gown, fastened my white handkerchief over my hair, and glided across the floor in my buckled slippers. I was Morjana, destroyer of villains, a magician of slippers and veils! I twirled around in rehearsal while Jessie tried to fasten her pillow around her stomach with a wicker belt, and Liz pulled the pom-poms from her shirt. Liz didn't know that she was in a play, and that might be a problem, but my sister and Jessie and I were ready for anything. We were actors, directors, producers too, and also, the ticket takers. We had to be everywhere at once. To let us know that he was really there, my father stepped backstage briefly. He would see us! He couldn't wait! He marveled at our costumes and wished us all broken legs. He conducted a mock interview for the *New York Times*. He treated us like celebrities, and we posed for him and giggled while he took our picture. The other adults had lined up noisily at the living room doors, so my sister, spotted and scabby, ran to greet them.

"Welcome to today's production of *Ali Baba and the Forty Thieves*, presented by the Town and Country Troupe!" She tore the construction paper tickets. I ran to hand out the programs.

Claire and Bob Bailey, bare-legged, sat together on the sofa, their freckled knees pressed close. My mother sat behind them, thin-lipped. She stared at them. Her sister sat beside her, with my uncle, and then those few other neighbors who had shown enthusiasm for our theatrical efforts. My father sat in the front row of folding chairs, telling jokes and making people laugh. The parents all had drinks they cradled on their bellies like baby animals and the air felt, for the first time in weeks, bright with pleasure and with something else—not amusement, really, but something quieter, a current that coursed between all the parents. They settled in together. My sister raised the small stage lights. Sally swung open her arms, a passive, perfect cave door of a girl. There was applause, and then silence. Not a mosquito sang. We had all the attention in the world. But our production did not turn out exactly as we had rehearsed and hoped. Liz kept tripping, and falling down, until finally, she shrieked and ran into the audience and climbed on to her mother's lap, and then everyone in the audience laughed so there was no going on with the show, even though we had barely begun. For weeks, I had imagined myself as Morjana, twirling in my blue gown as I rescued everyone from the thieves when they burst from their bottles and ran and Ali Baba finally spoke the magic words, and the immoveable Cave Door swung open at last to our cheers, and gold spilled across the stage. Instead, I stood on the stage, took my hankie from my hair and tossed it angrily— "It isn't over! And it's not supposed to be funny!" Sally quit being the Cave Door and flapped her arms up and down like a big bird. My sister shrugged. Liz kept crying. Suddenly, Bob Bailey stood up. He clapped his enormous tanned hands, and shouted out "Brava! Encore!" My father stood up quickly too and hugged everyone. My mother leapt to her feet—confused behind the two fathers who did not look at each other— and said, "Well, that's show business, kids!" She hurried out of the room for more drinks. Her body brushed up against the lamp and then against the doorframe. Bob Bailey looked after her. My father looked after her. The applause went on.

Our *Ali Baba and the Forty Thieves* production opened and closed quickly, a door itself, so many years ago but I can still see the slant of light across the cherry floorboards as we all took a bow in our tiny solid bodies . . . My father lifts me in his arms, and my foot catches inside his sweater and tears two buttons away. I feel the rip of wool, the pull and snag at the buckle of my shoe. I still smell the fruit and tang of my mother's Chanel perfume when she kissed me before bed and her earrings brushed against my face. I hear the kettle of water boiling on the stove, my father whistling in the dark as he polishes his dress shoes in the toasty kitchen. A wind rattles the branches above the driveway. I march through the kitchen in my nightgown and out the screen door. I pull hard on the rusted door of the Maid of the Mist, climb into the cracked driver's seat where no one but my father ever sits. I cannot see over the steering wheel. I put his key, which I have stolen, into the ignition. It is the right key, it fits perfectly, and I drive with a roar up into the air, over the houses, over the lawns, into the mist.

THE CURTAIN OF SUMMER has descended. Now it is night. The House on Hodge Road is a tomb of leaves and dead flies stirred by wind. No one knows yet what I have learned about mosquitoes, blood rituals, fertility, and the sliding shut of cave doors. No one knows if troubles of breathing can ever be resolved; no one knows what will happen next. My mother does not know she will one day die of ovarian cancer. She has simply completed another summer mystery—the girl, the gold watch, and everything! My father does not know that he will play music for the rest of his very long life, without her applause. He has just completed another summer gig. Mr. Bailey's swimming pool wears a shroud of black plastic. A hired worker will assess the breadth of limbs and the pertinent danger of trees. My sister turns in the twin bed against the wall, and the bedsprings squeak. She is mummified, a bandaged girl, bled, wrapped, and ready for adolescence. Mosquitoes squeal and careen against walls, and make a *tap tap* sound above my head, oblivious to seasons. Now my mother sleeps. My sister sleeps. My cousins sleep. I lie awake and wait for my father, who is not yet home.

I chew absently on a bit of garlic. Soon, there will be an arc of light across the flowered walls, a cough of his car's engine, and the crush of gravel beneath tires. When I hear him at last—the scrape of his dress shoes against the step and of his saxophone case on the stoop—I toss back the sweaty sheets and go to the window. He knocks, once, then again and again. I watch him turn and look out puzzled at the dark space of the lawn. He waits for my mother, but my mother does not come. Again, he knocks, a little louder. Still she does not come. I turn back toward the house, which still smells of burned paper and smoke. Had the shoe polish on the stove ignited and set the wallpaper on fire? Were my mother's distractions responsible for the flames? They traveled up the kitchen wall in a circus ribbon of light! I hadn't seen this happen, but I pictured my mother, a slipper in one hand, a cloth towel in the other, beating the flames furiously until finally, they went out and she stood alone, uncertain what to do next . . . I listen for my mother on the stairs, but there is not a sound. The rooms stretch and yawn around me, my sister yawns, and I know there is no one left for my father. There is no one to let him come home. I press my face against the screen of the window. I peer down at his slumped posture. He looks tired. I want to speak, to tell him, *soon, soon,* someone will come down the stairs to let him in! My mother will wake and hurry to him, my sister will stir and whisper, "Is that Dad?" and I will fall the long, inevitable distance into my own unconsciousness once the laughter and mutterings have ceased and my parents' bedroom door has shut firmly on their love, that permanent mystery of night. My parents will curl, I imagine, around one another in tenderness. They will breathe and turn together forever in their music of marriage and sleep.

The minutes drag away across the lawn toward the rabbit's cage, and my father sighs. I do not call down to him. I do not run to wake my mother. I watch him fumble for his keys. No, they're no good, keys are no good! *People open doors, not keys!* We both know this. My father walks back to the Maid of the Mist. He sits for several minutes in the front seat with the engine running, and then he drives away.

"Dad's gone," I say to my sister, loudly.

She sighs. "He'll be back. Please. Go to sleep."

I pull the curtain closed.

WHEN WE MOVED AWAY at summer's end, I orbited the house a last time, taking everything in as I always do whenever *the end* begins. There is my mother asleep in her underwear on a sofa, her hand fallen against the carpet, a mystery novel open across her face . . . there is my sister, ice packs on her thighs, a cloth around her bitten neck . . . there's my father's radio playing Benny Goodman, Chet Baker, Duke Ellington, the music filling all the rooms . . . the limb of Mr. Bailey's tree finally falling with a rustle across the hedge of our driveway . . . my cousins singing "the cat came back, they thought he was a goner!" . . . my mother rising and asking no one in particular, asking the air, "What's our poison tonight?" Around again. There is my mother falling down in the kitchen, or falling on the stairs, her chestnut hair turned silver . . . my cousins in their wedding gowns, walking their aisles, admiring their gold rings . . . my father carrying his sax case up and down a thousand stairs . . . my father carrying my mother . . . my parents clinging as though they are new young lovers dancing to a slow jazz tune . . . my mother in a hospital bed, her veins radiating the necessary poison . . . her pale body discovered. Her body, ashes. Now my mother calls to me, frightened, from somewhere else. She calls to me from some large and haunted space she cannot fathom, into that other space where I orbit alone in my middle age as her voice repeats itself in my words, these words I write: *Where is Melora? Is she all right? Where is she?*

I am standing on a wide sunlit lawn. I am seven years old. "Come on, kids!" my father yells, "Who wants to play with me? Don't any of you want to play? This is the great outdoors! Wake up, you little housemoles! Come on! You can't catch me!"

He wears his old sneakers and khakis and a frayed cotton sweater.

I will always remember him like this, while he grows older, frailer, and more breakable each year. He is jumping back and forth. He beckons to my sister, and to me, and to Liz and Jessie and Sally and Doogie who are all suddenly screaming and jumping back and forth too. There is a frenzy of delight and ecstatic movement, all the trucks are gone, the summer is suddenly unleashed, my father laughs breathlessly and cuts crazy zigzags across the grass and I watch as everyone begins to chase him. Sally and Doogie shriek and grab at the seat of my father's trousers. Jessie feints and dodges whenever he changes course. Liz falls and tumbles happily behind the others. My sister jogs along in his wake, smiling. My father darts around like this for a long time, pursued by children, hearing his own music, and then, he performs marvelous defeat, he does let them catch him after all. My father, captured at last! He falls dramatically on his playing field, bellowing beneath the weight of kids who buzz and crawl across his chest and unlace his sneakers and pin his arms in the grass. But of course, it's only an illusion. No one can ever really catch my father. Instead, he gathers *them* all up, he is holding them, he is hugging everyone to him, he can hug everyone at once, he is kissing and hugging and tickling everyone, there is enough laughter to last forever, and the noise of it all, of all this unexpected happiness, is as loud as forty thieves discovering riches, and brings my mother to the screen door where she stands quietly, holding her drink. My mother is a swaying orange blur behind the screen. She is an unfinished stroke of wild color and luck. "*Oh no, be careful!*" she calls out, her voice full of love and worry. "Don't get hurt! Don't let anyone end up hurt! No more trips to the hospital, please!" And when my father looks up, he sees me waiting alone, and shouts, "Hey! You! Little girl! What are you doing over there all by yourself? Why don't you want to play with us? Come on! *Let's go get her!*"

I don't move as my father runs toward me with open arms. I'm not sure what I am meant to do. I'm still not sure. What does it mean, after all, to be loved?

In a rush of sweat and cotton, my father sweeps me up in his arms and runs with me. I am the only one now. I cling to his neck. I feel his heart. We run faster and faster, my father with me, and no shade to this lawn that grows quiet and endless as we leave behind us the next minute, the next hour, the next life that approaches so quickly.

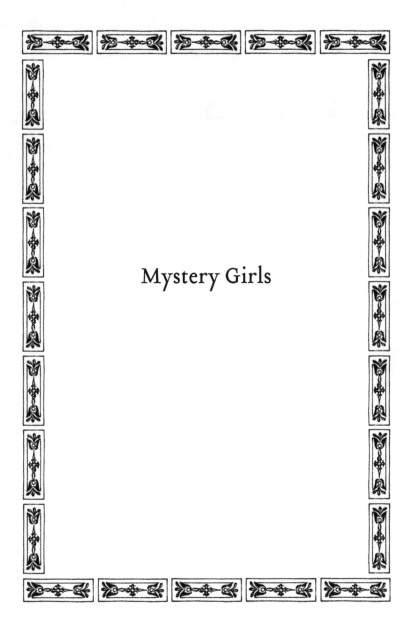

Mystery Girls

THE DANCE HALL at the Riverside Community Center was pitch-dark. Bodies collided. Limbs thrust. Mouths gasped. Girls bobbed up and down and gulped for air. The air was thick, dank. Older men we had never seen before played live music that vibrated the damp walls decorated with frames of faux gilt. The beat was steady, consuming, a tell-tale heart. Now thirteen and old enough to attend the Goddard Gaieties Society dances, we flailed eagerly on the dance floor. Sometimes two or three of the less mordant girls, guitars strapped onto their bodies, would stand in front of the band and start singing "Blowin' in the Wind" or "Here Comes the Sun," but then we were all plunged back into shadows and the steady beat resumed. Fueled by anonymity and by their stolen cigarettes, sweaty, long-haired boys prowled the crowds looking for the Mystery Girl. The Mystery Girl was their goal and their reward. Who was she? None of us knew, not even the Mystery Girl herself. That was to be part of the fun. The band would suddenly stop playing music and a follow spotlight would illuminate some swaying couple. The Mystery Girl was the one held captive in the boy's stiff arms. When this flash of light revealed the Mystery Girl's identity, she would cover her face and scream.

The boys chose their partners scattershot. The prize for dancing with a Mystery Girl could be significant. The lucky boy might win a transistor radio shaped like a car or like a truck. He would get to choose the radio-vehicle that he most wanted—Mercedes or Mack, convertible or pickup, boys have differing tastes—the same way that he had chosen his girl for the dance. The Mystery Girls won nothing. I discovered that if I made it as far as the dance floor with a boy, I was often selected by the beam of light as the Mystery Girl. The boys laughed when they found out I was the one. Then they raced off to claim their shiny radio and I was ordinary again. In time, I became more willful. I walked up to boys and said, "Do you want to dance with me? You should. I'm the Mystery

Girl. I guarantee it. If you choose me you're going to win a Mercedes Benz transistor radio."

Katie, who was deep into Piaget at that time, walked past me and said, "Your reasoning is seriously transductive, you know. You're going to have a *big* problem in later life."

I suspected she might be right.

Some other girls preferred not to dance at all and to make boys sulk in postures of macho defiance. These girls turned their backs on boys, provoking them toward shame and rage. We had heard that one of the boys—the one with the simian brow—had a terrible temper, and that he locked his girlfriend in the utility closet of his home whenever she disobeyed him. He kept his girlfriend trapped in the closet while he did whatever he pleased. He kept the key hidden in his pocket. We imagined she screamed for help inside the closet. But didn't his buddies also say that his girlfriend *liked* being trapped and that actually she *made* him do it? That she *liked* to be punished, and that he *liked* punishing, so they were meant for each other and thus, *in love?* Who could believe a story like that?

When the boys walked past us on the dance floor and jerked their heads in the direction of the exit, we followed them, nervously, out to the dark street. We went in girl gangs for protection. We linked arms as the boys put their new truck-radios on the sidewalk. They turned up the volume to drown out the voices of two beaded girls singing inside the Community Center, "Where Have All the Flowers Gone?" We tried not to think about the second-grade teacher who had been murdered one night in her apartment. A man had been waiting there for her in the darkness. He let her cat live, the only witness to the murder. We tried not to remember Kitty Genovese, whose fate was examined still in the city newspapers though over a decade had passed since the night she crawled bleeding toward her building, screaming for help. Supposedly, the thirty-eight neighbors who watched her from their windows as she staggered had done nothing. They hadn't thought it necessary. Stabbed and raped, Kitty died at the threshold of a doorway. The door had been locked. In psychology class, Miss Julie assigned us readings on the "bystander effect"—Genovese Syndrome—and articles in which the man who murdered Kitty confessed to police that he'd chosen her from the crowd entirely at random. He was simply in the mood to stab an innocent girl to death. Kitty did not know that she was the chosen one until it was too late.

On the street, we pushed aside these thoughts when the boys from the dance hall faced us. Their hands groped in their trouser pockets.

"Do any of you Mystery Girls like grass?"

For flirtations with green grass, we headed down to the East River boardwalk on sunny days. We ran from the Brearley School and along the promenade, stepped up onto benches, and tossed our book bags over the iron spiked fences that separated us from small raised plots of grass. We were always careful not to disturb the homeless men that slept on the benches under blankets of cardboard or to put our foot accidentally through the rotting wood slats and rip our blue knee socks. When we stepped onto the tiny estates, they proved to be mostly brown weeds and piles of dirt adorned with bottle caps, beer cans, candy wrappers, and broken glass. We sat cross-legged, our pleated uniforms spread artfully and politely over our knees. On our little patches of grass, we felt intimate with Nature. Sometimes, our desire for Nature took us on walks from the East Side to the West Side through Central Park along paths that wound between lawns and ball fields, but we avoided the shadows of the park at dusk so we would not attract thugs. Sensible, we also avoided the bronze statue of Alice sitting in a grove with all the creatures of Wonderland—the worried rabbit with his watch, the Cheshire cat, and the duck—each one a monument to distant childhood. The Mad Hatter grinned nearby. Once, we had held on tightly to Alice's outstretched polished finger, which pointed toward some invisible, fantastic realm; we sat happily and safely in her lap, looking out at the world. But soon, the sun heated the statue's metal and we had scalded our bottoms and run to our mothers, screaming. Years later, we looked out across the lake toward Belvedere Castle situated on a high ledge on the far side of the water like a medieval beacon, all its windows boarded and barred. Sometimes we heard the engines of motorcycles and saw gangs of boys smoking cigarettes on the castle's old terrace. The boys exchanged objects we could not identify from our opposite shore. Once we saw several large boys surround a smaller figure they shoved and slapped repeatedly. Educated, we said nothing and hurried from the park.

Every few months a stranger phoned the high school and threatened to blow up the building and all of the girls in it. We were evacuated immediately. We knew the drill. Bomb drills were silent, smooth, and efficient. Whispering, we waited outside on the boardwalk with our teachers while policemen and firemen searched the thirteen stories of the school with guns, and police dogs sniffed the lockers for the scent of hidden bombs. Which girl, we wondered, was the single target among six hundred? Despite our matching ironed uniforms and oxford shoes, some girls did stand out. Egalitarian, we insisted that we were all exactly alike, and that bomb threats were—as our mothers told us—someone's sick plea for attention. But there were hushed rumors. Somewhere, someone longed for the death of *one* girl. She was chosen from among us all for no particular reason, an eighth- or ninth-grader or a girl even younger, an innocent who was busy conjugating Latin verbs, braiding lanyards, and practicing scales on her cello. This fact kept us quiet as we stood beside the river and waited for someone to tell us we were safe.

FIELD DAY WAS an excursion from the building that all of us welcomed— an ordinary and peaceful expulsion of girls into a verdant world. We boarded the school buses happily and traveled to Randall's Island to compete. True, some girls' skills were more suited to a grassless realm—

those girls who were awkward, preoccupied, underweight or overweight, and had mastered only certain athletic feats to ensure basic survival. These were girls who heard the word "island" and thought, *Lord of the Flies.* These girls—and I was among them, my only athletic feat the headstand—remained on the sidelines. We kept scores and did nothing to distinguish ourselves. We remained unsung. But several girls had physical prowess. Lisa leapt over the high jump bars set at five feet; Stacy ran the dash in twelve seconds; Danielle threw a shot put forty-seven feet through the air. We saw what a little lawn could do for a girl. Giddily, we remembered our hero Gloria Steinem, so hip and sassy in Assembly Hall on Speaker Day as she swayed in her sexy purple leotard and blue jeans, tossed her long beautiful hair, cracked jokes from behind her tinted glasses about men who would try to stop us from living our lives. Over our thunderous applause and cheers, she shouted, *We will stand together, girls! Don't ever forget, we are stronger than they are! We can do anything!* And indeed, we had all stood together filled with hope in our immediate ovation for Gloria. On Field Day, we gathered in the grass around our own school champions alive in their female super-bodies. We cheered and waved our red-and-white gym belts over our heads. When the whistle sounded and Miss King placed ribbons on the winners, I wished I was one of them and could wear my own purple ribbon of victory. But I stomped and clapped in rhythm with all the girls: Miya, Lydia, Laura, Lizzie, Diana, Katie, Abby, Sarah, Monique, Maria, Heather, Claudia, Sydney, Virginia. I liked to sing with them in unison our favorite school bus song. "We're Brearley born and Brearley bred! And when we *die,* we're Brearley *dead!*"

In drama class, we practiced theater exercises for our teacher, Mr. Ennis. Mr. Ennis was young, athletic, and had ice-gray eyes. He wore jeans and work boots and shirts slightly unbuttoned to reveal the dark hair on his chest. He had a gold earring in one ear. He kept his hair messy. Mr. E. taught us the Attention Exercise in which each girl was to capture his attention onstage with a gesture that would distinguish her from the rest. She might salute, or pick her nose, or turn her back while all the other girls twirled and jumped around. Standing completely frozen proved to be an effective strategy for gaining Mr. E.'s attention. He would point at a completely motionless girl and shout from his seat at the back of the theater, "Look there! She's the one!" He never pointed at me. I fidgeted; I blended in. Then, we moved on to the Trust exercise. For the Trust exercise we all gathered together beside Mr. E. and looked up to the stage, ready. There, a single girl would take deep breaths and prepare herself to fall blindly backward off of the stage's edge and into our waiting arms. We had no idea how to catch falling girls or what they might feel like, but the task proved to be a simple one when we all stood together, just as Gloria Steinem had encouraged us to do. The bodies of the girls were as light as beanbags. Mr. E., however, declined to fall backward into our arms when I asked him to complete the Trust exercise too. I liked the idea, but he did not.

Sometimes, Mr. E. handed out scripts. We read aloud scenes from *Lysistrata* and *Eurydice* and *Alcestis*. We read from *The Women* and from *Antigone*. We all hoped to play the lead female roles, of course, but casting choices could be made only by Mr. E. The competitive spirit was high. I viewed our auditions as my best shot at applause, a theatrical Field Day. I felt that even I could rise to the occasion if I had the spotlight. I would throw the discus as far as I wanted—dramatically speaking, that is—if I won the starring role. If nothing else, I wouldn't have to bribe boys for attention anymore with transistor radios shaped like Mack trucks and cars. Maybe I *could* do anything, Gloria! Why *couldn't* we girls just choose the parts we wanted to play? Why did he choose? Why did we have to be chosen at all?

"You girls all have such beautiful hair!" Mr. Ennis said enthusiastically and applauded when we had each completed our dramatic reading. I narrowed my eyes at him, but he continued. "You are all leading ladies!

I sure would like to cast you all!" We clutched our scripts in our laps and blushed, embarrassed for Mr. E. or for ourselves, although we were all proud of our hair. We didn't think until later about the long-haired girls who had been shot in the front seat of a car after their night at a discothèque out past Pelham Bay, so very far away from us we believed. But we knew that there had been more girls wounded or killed after that in parked cars, just like the first two. Their names appeared every few months in the news.

Police reported that they had no information about the serial killer. They did, however, mention the fact of the girls' long dark hair. We heard the girls' hair might actually have provoked the killer's psychosis. Newsmen wondered if girls' hair—its length, its brunette color, its style (ponytail or bangs, curled or straight) might become an essential clue, a braid of evidence a detective might unravel, like the bald detective in *Kojak*, a show my mother watched at night on TV. Some girls at school cut their hair. Some girls tried new styles. Discreetly, we talked about dyeing. Police hoped that long-haired girls could point them to the real killer. So far, we knew, only one girl of five attacked had survived and been able to describe the man, but only as a movement to the side of the car, a figure that reached into a paper bag and crouched down like an animal. She glimpsed him moments before her friend cried out and the car's windows shattered. The killer was described in the news as a curly-haired man with fat cheeks and a .44 caliber revolver. No further details. How many men had curly hair and fat cheeks? Half of the men in the city! We studied an artist's rendering of the serial murderer printed on the front page of the paper. The first time I saw his sketched face, I thought he looked like a little boy, squirrely and unformed, and said so. Surely, we were safe from him! None of the girls agreed with me. And then the drawings began to change. With each crime, the drawings in the newspapers became more substantive, more detailed. The killer seemed to age. Were the artists becoming more skilled? Were eyewitnesses changing their stories? Were witnesses completely unreliable? Maybe the murderer transformed himself with each crime he committed. First, the portraits of him had been spare and simple. They depicted a man with no eyebrows. A few crimes later, his brows were arched and high. First, he had been fat. Then he was very thin. His cheeks weren't chubby; they were hollow. He had no neck. Then he had wide shoulders. In one sketch he appeared to be white. In another he looked Latino. Then he looked white again. In October his eyes were small and round, the eyes of an adolescent. By January, they were large and empty. His crimes, we guessed, would never be solved.

DURING THE DAYS spent safely inside the Brearley School, our thirteen-story tower by the river, we wrote our papers on the brush techniques in J. M. W. Turner's *Venice* series. We composed our Petrarchan Sonnets. We performed our cello recitals, a production of *Wonderful Town*, and a radio play of "The Waste Land." We pondered the mystery of "pi"—a number irrational, unquantifiable, and infinite. Could we solve a problem that both multiplied and divided Infinity? We completed our oil paintings for an exhibition of the school's Kuntz Collection— "pronounced Koontz," our teachers said wearily—and applied Piaget's developmental stage theories to the narrators of *Frankenstein* and of William Faulkner's *As I Lay Dying*. In dance class, we staged an Elizabethan masque. In Classics, we read *The Homeric Hymn to Demeter*. We studied the ancient Eleusinian Mysteries and initiations into the cult of the goddess. And at lunch in the cafeteria, we shared pages from the books our mothers said we were not allowed to read—*The Godfather, A Clockwork Orange,* and *One Flew over the Cuckoo's Nest*. Then, filled with forbidden stories of abductions, rapes and demons, slaughters, and prisons, we began our journey home.

Some girls hailed taxis, and sat slumped in the back seat, to hide from the taxi driver's rearview mirror. The mothers would not let us see the new movie in town—*Taxi Driver*—despite our indignant cries, "Jodie Foster is in it!" But we saw the posters. There was our beloved Jodie in stacked heels, tiny shorts, and black mascara, a hat's brim flopped over her brow. DeNiro posed as Travis Bickle with his dark glasses, leather jacket, and Mohawk. We knew about the way Bickle watched his passengers in the mirror of his taxicab. His eyes revealed nothing of his madness or his visions of massacre. Solemnly, we waved goodbye to the girls who got into taxicabs. Then we began to follow the route between school and home our mothers had mapped for us.

We steered clear of Carl Schurz Park. The park had once been our heaven, perfect for our lunch-hour meals, until the day a man in dark glasses had sat down cross-legged beside us on the grass. "Where do you girls go to school?" he had asked, pleasantly. "I like your uniforms a lot. Do you have to wear those all the time?" And we were not to linger at the penny-candy store on East End either, where we liked to gather between classes to kill time and suck on hard candy and Twizzlers. We could no longer head over to Dorian's Red Hand for a burger and Coke and the chance to meet some handsome preppies, or to The Met for the afternoon—not since that incident with the photographer who stopped us on the grand steps, lifted his camera in his hands and said, "I'm looking for pretty models for a project in my studio and you girls would be perfect. Would any of you like to be models?"

After the murderer shot his seventh victim in March, a student on her way home from school, the mothers said we would never walk home alone from school again. We felt the girl had been our own classmate hurrying from the subway, cradling her schoolbooks in her arms. We supposed she hadn't been thinking about the killer at all because he usually hunted couples on stoops or in parked cars. When the stranger stepped out of the shadows and lifted his arm from behind his back, the girl instinctively raised her schoolbooks to cover her face. But the books did not save her. We tried not to think about that as we walked, our knapsacks packed with the heavy volumes we carried for blocks each day. Ovid. Homer. Dante. Shakespeare. Milton. Blake. What did they matter?

I turned my back on the beautiful, darkening tree-lined side street not yet lit by evening lanterns. I hurried into my building, ran up the stairs, and locked myself into the fourth-floor apartment. There were three gold locks on the front door and a brass sliding chain—someone would have to break that chain to get inside by lifting a large violent foot and stomping the metal to pieces, and that would be quite noisy and the noise would alert the neighbors, who would call for help because that's what neighbors do. At least, that's what Kitty had believed. My mother—still at her office, but vigilant and worried—left instructions for me on the dining table.

Don't answer the doorbell. If someone knocks, turn off all the lights. Don't move.

The city felt too small for girls. Like a dark closet we couldn't escape.

Four stories down behind the buildings, tiny gardens grew. Small seeds gradually matured into sturdy, urban plants with long rubbery leaves that waved like panicked arms. In these garden plots—which I could not see but could imagine—the roots of trees spread beneath concrete garden paths and began to push the concrete up in cracked lumps of mortar and dirt. From my bedroom window, I could see the tops of the trees as they brushed up against the fire escapes. Awake in my bed, I stared out at all the limbs and listened to a woman scream in one of the gardens. Hers was a deep, full-throated voice that climbed in its hysteria around 3:00 or 4:00 a.m., on weekends. Although there were no other sounds—no shouts, no scuffles, no shatters of glass—the woman's screams rose up as long wails of pain, desperation, and then, of surrender. "He's killing me! He's killing me!" I slid under the blankets in the dark and waited for more. "Stop killing me, you bastard! Stop killing me! Oh god, you're going to kill me again! How many times are you going to kill me?" I tried to picture her face—young, delicate, stricken—but her face kept changing in my mind. Only her screams were real. The trees swayed and eventually, the woman fell silent until the following weekend, when she screamed again.

Gradually, my blood went cold.

WE WANTED TO GO WILD. We wanted to swivel our hips and feel a shower of glittering snowflakes fall on our hot skin. We wanted to feel a sexual weather sent down from a flashing disco heaven. Studio 54 sparkled in midtown Manhattan shiny and new, ready to open its doors to us. We would line up outside the velvet rope in our flimsy spring dresses; we would try to keep our balance in our new high-heeled shoes as we waited; we would whisper the secret passwords that would let us slip by the men that barred our entry to the club. Celebrities would surround us. The music would consume us. But no, we understood that this would never happen. We were not *allowed* to go to Studio 54 where dealers and drunks cut cocaine with credit cards and chose the girls they would follow through the city or assault in the restrooms, our mothers said. Our sophomore prom in May would instead be held in the ballroom of the Pierre Hotel, and we would not attend without a date to escort us, one of the fine young men available to us through the Afterschool Activities Program. We each hoped one of them would call and extend a proper invitation—maybe Robert, a Dalton boy with a beautiful tenor voice, or maybe Ted, who had emerged from a silver papier-mâché forest of sweet musk-roses, mayflowers, and eglantine bathed in false moonlight in the spring Interschool production of *A Midsummer Night's Dream*. He scattered sequins over his Fairy Queen and sent a hairy beast into her arms to punish her wandering attentions. I even spent one evening with Ted on the front stoop of my building, my shoulder pressed against his, his knee pressed against mine. Couples walked bravely down the street toward the river and I barely noticed that it was getting dark, the shadows felt so benign on a warm spring night. Ted did not look quite as handsome as he had in the play, but maybe reality could be better than theater. It was possible. Ted's blond hair fell over one eye. He laughed with only one side of his mouth. His nose was faintly freckled. He un-buttoned the collar of his shirt and I could see his smooth, tanned chest and a small Saint Christopher medal hanging on a gold chain around his neck. I had just reached over to touch the medal and ask, "Where did you get that?" when my mother opened the front door of the building and waved one of her arms outside frantically, without actually stepping outside herself.

"What are you doing? What are you thinking?" she called through the open door. "Do you have any idea what is going on in this city right now? No stoops. Come inside."

Ted stood up quickly, apologized, excused himself politely, and headed home. I watched him walk down the street. Impossibly tall, he strolled with a boyish swing in his step. I doubted he would ask me to the prom. That left only George, who had played the role of the hairy beast. He had shaken his long, furred ears and pawed the stage-earth with such conviction that even in his inhuman costume and wild makeup, he seemed real. No one wanted to go to the prom with George.

"You're blighting my life," I told my mother.

I anticipated some reply to this, but none came as she watched me flounce past her into the building. Later, she would tell me, again, the story about the girl she had once known in high school who was raped by a boy she'd known well—or whom she had thought she knew well. At first, he had seemed to be a gentleman, polite and charming and ad-mired by many. After the rape, when the girl was *permanently changed,* my mother said, and the boy was inexplicably *not arrested* and simply continued to live his life freely, unpunished for his crime, the girl's fa-ther tried to kill the boy himself. The father had been a handsome and admired young man once too, but he'd never hurt anyone. He was a quiet person, reserved. Yet he chased the boy with a hatchet, my mother told me. Was there a hint of pride in her tone? I pictured the father of her story wielding the hatchet, running down lanes or across lawns in my mother's hometown in the Midwest. He hadn't slept in nights, and there were shadows of rage and anguish beneath his eyes. He ran past white clapboard houses and yapping terriers and over gravel driveways in pursuit of the boy who had raped his daughter. I wondered how far it was possible for a powerful and devastated man to run while also carrying a hatchet and if he ran in daylight or in darkness to find his prey, but in my imagination, he just kept on running, pursuing justice, until he became only a tiny speck and then disappeared. I couldn't remember what happened next. I didn't think it mattered. The important part of her story was done.

On the night of the prom, our mothers wouldn't sleep. They had watched us hurry out together in our gowns and they would wait for us to get back safely. The mothers had told us to stay on the lit avenues, and not to head home from the prom near the trees, but they doubted we had paid any attention. They would lie with their eyes open wide and wait for us to call, or for the sound of our key turning each of the locks on the door but hearing instead the usual late-night sirens that announced terrible news for someone. Did they remind us not to walk alone and to stay with all the other girls when the dance was done? Did they remind us not to wander near Central Park with its blood-black grass rippling like water in the rising wind? Had they given us enough money to buy our way back home in case something went terribly wrong? They were always grieving for their daughters. They couldn't help it.

"Worry is their rite," Katie concluded as we all slipped into a single taxi. We understood that fear was lowered slowly down to the mothers in the bottomless wells of myth. We pictured Persephone as she appeared in our *History of Art*, sculpted and naked in Bernini's marble, her arms flung open, her hair still loose and wild from a day spent gathering flowers in the fields, her mouth open as she tried to escape the arms of Hades. His fingers dug deeply into her body. I imagined the earth splitting open, the monster and his immortal horses rising up from the cloven rock, then the quick abduction. And she was gone. The earth closed again while her mother wept. I imagined too the wailing, the searching, the neglected fields dying around Demeter as she mourned. Obviously, our mothers couldn't understand that we were going to the sophomore prom or that there was no such thing as Hell or that we carried enough money to take a taxi safely home. *Make sure the driver is old,* our mothers cautioned. For the mothers, we supposed, grief would always be the infinite plan of the gods. Nobody wins. Half the world was dying.

But maybe my mother was right, I thought as I headed out the door to the dance. Maybe we wanted too much to prove we were fearless. Secretly, I remembered my mother trembled when she heard on the news in April that another young couple had been killed—a dark-haired girl and her boyfriend. Police identified the .44 caliber gun again as the weapon. I pictured the killer's empty eyes, his pudgy hollow cheeks, his broad narrow shoulders, his dark light skin as he stalked girls and shifted his shape, multiplying. In their photograph on the front page after the double homicide, the young couple seemed to me to be in love. They both were dressed up and smiling. I imagined they had been headed for a dance. The girl was a hopeful actress, my mother had told me. She shook her head sadly. And the boy, I thought, was handsome and wholesome, a bit like the Kennedy boy. Maybe the couple had posed together for their mothers' Polaroid cameras and for posterity, just as we had posed for our mothers' cameras before heading to the prom. We blinked at the sudden flash of light. After that, we barely saw what we were doing or where we were going.

The sidewalks were wet from a light rain. We hitched our gowns above our knees to protect our dresses' hems from puddles. Katie wore an emerald-green gown that flared into a green fan, a mermaid's tail; Abby wore a straight pale-blue shift; I wore a faintly pink dress and pink buckled slippers that fell off when I stepped across the curb in front of the Pierre. Beneath gold lamps and silver streamers and crystal chandeliers in the ballroom of the hotel, and with the noble postures of almost-adults we'd practiced years ago at Barclay's Ballroom Dancing School, we finally waltzed in the arms of the boys. Barclay's was far behind us, yet somehow the little flourishes of elegance returned to us easily: the right hand tips delicately, invitingly to the right; the chin lowers shyly to the left; the eyes glance up every now and then. The boys, we thought, achieved a distinguished disarray of bow ties and unbuttoned sleeves and lumpy cummerbunds. The band played medleys of romantic and rock tunes to keep everyone on their feet. I danced a little with Ted who looked princely in his tuxedo, I thought, and after each dance, we sat together at a table in the ballroom with the other *couples* (we were couples!)—Robert and Abby, George and Katie—and spooned angel food cake into our mouths. But when we tried to think of conversations we might have with these boys, nothing interesting came to mind and so the night dragged on as we smiled at each other uncomfortably. Katie wondered who would dance with her. George wondered if it was true that girls all menstruate at the same time. Ted changed the subject. The band played "It's a Miracle," and Robert wondered if we should just leave.

"Why don't we wait until this song has ended?" Ted said and smiled at me.

When midnight approached, our secret supply of Muscadet ran out, and the band abandoned Barry Manilow for Billy Joel's "Ain't No Crime," the park suddenly seemed to us like an adventure and an excellent idea. We left the hotel and ran across the avenue with the boys. George loped a little in drunk and comic imitation of his hairy beast performance. He paused to paw at a sewer grate and then at a manhole cover out of which gushed a hot plume of steam. He barely dodged a speeding taxi. The driver shook a fist and drove on. We hardly worried about our dresses, although the hems dragged in the gutter, and the straps already slipped from our shoulders. We stumbled over to benches beside the stone wall that divided the park from the street. There at last we kissed the boys.

We kissed them tentatively at first, then confidently, inspired by the invisible forces of their desire. When the kissing improved and we felt the unfamiliar, hard male bodies press us back down against the wooden benches, we tried to adjust our gowns or maybe just catch the scent of spring drifting over the park's wall from a wide, open field, but a scent of grass mingled instead in our nostrils with odors of exhaust, city garbage, male sweat, and something fetid. The benches were sticky. Lightning flashed once behind the hotel. The rain, and kissing, started again. This wasn't just kissing. This was serious. This was *really happening.* We froze. Were we still all there together? Could we still hear each other's gasps and the little rips of our dresses? Were we actually *alone?* We knew at once that we shouldn't be out there at the edge of the park, vulnerable, like all those girls before they were killed. Every stranger that walked past the park might be *him.* Our hearts raced. We felt hands pull up our slips and slide between our legs. We pushed them away. We heard whispers in our ears. "You have beautiful hair." We tried to remember the Trust exercise, the best way to fall freely into someone's arms, but we could not do it. It was too late. A stranger approached, stopped to stare, and then passed us by. But then there was another, and another after that, the strangers kept loping forward in the rain, there were more and more of them rising up in plumes from the cracks and fissures in the stone, an endless legion of men dividing and multiplying into Infinity.

We shivered, our flesh exposed. We twisted in the arms of the boys and tried to escape. They laughed and held us down. I thought of the girl who was permanently changed, of the father running for justice with a hatchet in his hands. I grabbed Ted's St. Christopher medal and tugged on it as hard as I could.

"What's wrong?" he said, startled, sitting up. Could the other girls hear me? Where were they? I couldn't hear them anymore at all. We did not want to be singled out and alone in the dark! We did not want to be chosen as the One! We did not want to become a Mystery Girl.

"*I am not a women-hater*," the killer had written in a neatly printed note he left at the scene of a crime.

But if not a woman-hater, what *was* he?

The Monster Beelzebub.

Beelzeboul. Prince of the Demons. Lord of the Flies.

I waited for a figure to appear from beneath the shroud of trees.

IN JULY, my mother hoped to have all of the windows in the apartment barred. Soon, workers would install metal gates that would block the views of the summer trees. There would be locks with combinations and tiny keys, and my mother would place the keys around the apartment on shelves, or hang them on hooks, or maybe keep them in the porcelain soup tureen she had inherited from her mother who had also inherited it from *her* mother. One afternoon, I waited alone in the apartment for my mother's return. I drifted restlessly from room to room. Soon, any slant of sunlight would shift and vanish behind the inevitable bars, and the green leaves would look patchy and brief. After the installation of bars, I would have to make the impossible choice between two worlds. *You can choose the life you want!* Gloria Steinem had shouted to us in the auditorium during our ovation for her. This couldn't be the kind of choice she had meant. I wanted a choice that could change everything.

I looked out of the unobstructed windows for the last time. Then I changed into a summer dress, applied a lipstick of my mother's, slipped into my heeled sandals, and stepped out into the city's killing heat. I didn't bother to lock the door of the apartment behind me. I scribbled no note of explanation for my mother to find when she returned from work. These things did not matter to me. I knew I would not be back until long after dark, when the air cooled just a little and the hydrants—gushing water onto the hot pavements outside the buildings—were capped again, and the streetlamps were on, and the bridges shone gold across the rivers. I didn't walk far, but where I pleased. I went first to the penny-candy store, then down to the playground where I used to hide in the cinderblock princess castle and peer out from its tower, and then on past the rocket ship slide and jungle gyms. From the boardwalk, I stared out across the river to the lighthouse on the opposite island. Boys skateboarded past me. A few whistled at me, one gestured rudely, but nothing more. The city seemed especially bright to me, like a light bulb just before it goes out. I didn't know that within twenty-four hours, there would be a sudden strike of lightning to some Hudson River sub-station, and when the unexpected energy surged in search of another outlet, a second flash would strike, transmission lines would fail, power limits would be exceeded. There would be a full collapse of the intricate electrical currents that mapped the city in hidden arteries and veins. Blackout. And then would come the swift and rolling wave of Darkness, an enormous shadow cast across the island, and the underground world about which I knew nothing would finally rise, furious and on fire, into streets I'd never seen. But not yet. I watched for predators behind me, just as we had all been taught to do. If they were behind me, their images would be reflected in the black windows of the parked cars. I steered away from the high school's pier and the shapes of men gathered be-neath it. The tips of their cigarettes glowed in the shadows. No preda-tors appeared. Maybe I had conquered the villains with my long stride, loose hair, and clenched fists? Brearley born! Brearley bred! So why was it that when I returned safely and miraculously *home*, chewing on fruit candy, there were four police cars parked at odd angles in the street outside the brownstone, the red and amber lights spinning? Why was my mother on the curb, sobbing, while a policeman with a notebook tried to get her attention? Why was she suddenly screaming and running toward me with her arms stretched out, her hair a tangle of mythic distress? Her cheeks flamed with rage or grief. I wanted to run. This apparition flying toward me down the street was not my mother.

"How could you do this? How could you do this to your mother?"

I imagined the windows of the brownstones opened. All of the neighbors listened. They peered down from the apartment windows into the street below as though they peered down a bottomless well in which my mother's cries echoed. They would see my mother hurl herself against me. I would fail to catch her falling body. They would watch us stagger in the street, two tiny beings tangled in each other's arms. The neighbors too would wonder, as suddenly I wondered guiltily myself, *How could she have done this to her mother?*

"There was a man trying to kill me!" I exclaimed just before she reached me. She stopped and stared at me. Her sobs ceased immediately. I kept on. "There was a man, on the fire escape, he tried to open the window to our apartment, he saw me and said he was going to rape me and kill me, so I ran away, I left the apartment, I ran outside, I didn't know what to do, I'm sorry! I'm sorry!"

My mother gasped then and pulled me down into a long embrace. "You poor baby," she said into my hair.

"Excuse me." An officer cleared his throat and approached us. He didn't look familiar, but young, eager. He had a notebook and pencil in hand. "Miss, what did this man who threatened you look like? Could you describe him for me, for the record?"

"Yes." I paused, and glanced at my mother. "He was ordinary."

"What does *ordinary* look like? For the police report. You understand, Miss?"

"Describe the perp for the officer," my mother said.

"He looked like everybody. I mean, like anybody."

The officer seemed annoyed. "Can you describe 'anybody' in more detail?"

My mother took my hand reassuringly. I said, "Of course I can."

Later, when my mother and I sat in the apartment and stared at the television news, she did not tell me again the story about the girl who was permanently changed, or about the father who finally took justice into his own hands. And she did not speak of the most recent shooting, but I knew about it. On the night of her high school graduation, a beautiful girl and her escort had been shot by the serial killer after they left a city dance hall. Unlike the others, the girl and boy both managed to survive. I imagined the girl staggered from the car shouting for someone, for anyone, to help her, *please, God, please* and I saw her fall into the street, bleeding. She couldn't stand up. She saw the light of the dance hall. So she started to crawl. Who helped her? The reports didn't say. Official witnesses to the shooting said only that they had seen the killer divide suddenly into two men, one dark and one light, and then escape in opposite directions simultaneously, one man in a vehicle and one man on foot, and then both murderers had vanished into the rain. But that couldn't be true, I thought. Maybe the two men were accomplices. Or the witnesses were seeing double. Were they speculators or witnesses, turning the unbearable facts to fictions they could bear? Telling stories . . . was that the key? I considered the bars and locks that would arrive the following afternoon to seal me permanently inside the apartment. I knew the story I'd given the police provided a poor description of the man on the fire escape. It had all happened so fast. I could have reported that the man was unique. He had worn ostrich feathers and had a parrot wired to his shoulder. But I had not. Instead I'd said, with a surge of confidence and voluptuous clarity, that the man I saw had fat cheeks and curly hair. He wore work boots and a shirt unbuttoned at the collar. He was young, with broad shoulders. He was white. His eyes were empty. He had looked into my eyes and I had felt pulled, for a moment, down into his realm. But I escaped to the surface to tell my story. I could identify his face perfectly, I said—so perfectly in fact, that secretly I believed I *had* actually seen his face—the face of a creature let loose from a dim corner of my mind. I saw him as he climbed toward me through my long hair. He was mine. He was real.

The police found the man at midnight. He rested on a patch of ruined grass beside the boardwalk. Calmly, he looked across the river. Maybe he smoked a joint. I imagined his face was stunned and then angry when the policemen drew their weapons, hauled him to his feet and shoved him—"Hey!" he said, "It's just grass, guys!"—and handcuffed him. They brought him in a police car to my doorstep. Immediately, I was summoned down to the street. There, the officers presented the captured man to me. The handcuffed fellow before me kept his gaze down. His shoulders were hunched—maybe he was crying?—and I could see that he was sweating heavily. He was a youngish man, a little older than I had pictured. He wore a soft, short-sleeved shirt, untucked and open. His delicate wrists were half-hidden under leather bracelets. He wore canvas shoes—not work boots, as I had recalled so precisely for the policemen, but black high-tops with the laces open and the tongues hanging out. The police had gotten my boot detail wrong. But the high-tops were a lot better. One officer stood beside the man near the front stoop of my brownstone. Two more officers flanked the steps of the building, barring him from the entrance. Their hands rested lightly on their guns. Neighbors stepped out of other buildings on the block, curious about what they might witness on a street usually so quiet at night, and they began to gather around us as an audience. Was the woman from the garden somewhere near me? She no longer screamed at night, or I no longer heard her. I supposed she had been killed for the final time. But if she was in this crowd now, I was certain I would recognize her immediately, the fear and desperation etched permanently into her cheeks and the hope in her eyes nearly snuffed out. I thought she might feel the current between us and signal to me, or cover her face with grateful hands. But when I looked for the one I wanted, I couldn't find her. The faces around me all seemed to blend together. I would never pick her out of the crowd. She would always be a mystery.

I felt dizzy. My mother stepped onto the front stoop behind me, her cheeks and her eyes slightly swollen. I shivered. The heat was scorching.

"Miss," the officer spoke and then shoved the cuffed man roughly toward me. He stumbled, but still, he wouldn't look up. "Do you recognize this man? Is he the one?"

I heard a loud rushing in my ears. Suddenly I felt I was back at school with the girls and we were all gathered safely in the auditorium, standing together, shouting and stomping our feet and cheering in one thunderous, overpowering ovation.

But all the girls were gone. I was alone.

I noticed that the hydrant in front of the building was still open and flowing weakly. A dark liquid streamed into the gutter and into the cracks of the sidewalk. Wide pools spread across the pavement toward me. The light of the police car kept spinning, casting its shade across my vision. Everything was bathed in red.

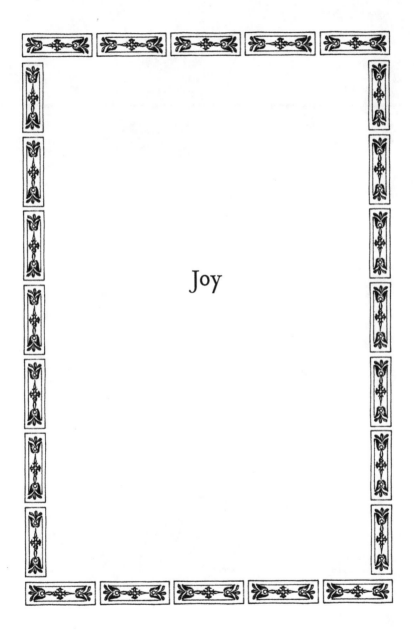

Joy

T HERE WAS A LADDER, and above the ladder, an open door.
I saw my cousin peering down at me. She beckoned for me to climb up. The barn below, where I hesitated, was dank and musty, long empty of animals and in the first apparent stages of decay. At one end of the barn, morning sunlight shone through the top of a half-opened door, and at the other end as well, the day still there, reachable and easy. I stood in a dark center.

"Come on!" Jessica said. She had managed the ascent up the ladder by herself.

I climbed slowly, watching my own hands. Jessica reached for my arms and pulled me over the lip of the barn floor. The air smelled so sweet. The sweetness was too much, a solid thing that cloaked our bodies, and we rolled through the rotting hay, flung it at one another, burrowed into it laughing, and my head ached with the scent. There was a visible soft cloud of yellow and blue fuzz that could be pulled deep into the body and held. Jessica pried open the loft window, which swung out, letting the sunlight and fresh air inside. The hay turned gold instead of gray, and there was a rush of wings as barn swallows started to dart and fly around us. There were dozens of them diving toward the light, out into the open air and then back in again. My uncle called up to us from the ordinary gravel far below, "What are you kids doing?" We lay on our stomachs at the window and stared at him. From our view up there, he looked like a boy in his proper shirt and pressed jeans, a city boy left out of all the fun. "Lunch is ready," he called to us and waved. He headed back toward the house, singing.

I have concluded another year, and I wake each day to that sweet-smelling memory that won't quit me as so many of my thoughts have done. The memory comes to me for some reason I feel I must grab onto, before it's too late. It was summer or spring. The barn was adjacent to a house on a road in upstate New York. It was early in the day, and early in the 1960s. Or it was none of these things at all. But I believe that the morning in the loft was the first time in my life that I felt joy. I looked out of the loft window at the morning and thought, I am happier now than I have ever been in the *five long years* of my life, and I will remember this, always.

Once at a cocktail party, I heard a graying man sigh and remark to his guests, "Joy is not something that children are capable of feeling. Joy is an old people's illness." That frightened me, the notion that the best of human response to being alive, to being human, would come only near the end of living in the quick descent to dust. And that the intensity, arriving so late, would feel like an unjust invasion, a final illness foisted upon illness, as a last extinguishing blow. I think he was wrong and that joy begins when the mind first reels at the power of the senses; when the body trembles and whispers a word you can taste and let spill from your lips again and again, declaring, *Now. This. Always.*

I was five. But I was not five. I was myself. This message is sent to me along that delicate but durable circuit established long ago in the hayloft; it is sent into my dreams, and into my consciousness each day as my boyfriend, the builder, brews coffee and showers. He is always up early, eager to see the moment when dark turns to light, and to prepare himself for his day's tasks. He is building a barn, steadily, neatly, without hesitation, lining up beams for the floor of the loft. But first come his rituals of washing, eating, praying, and sometimes singing in the kitchen songs about bears, deer, and coyotes dancing on the hillside. Sometimes he makes phone calls to connect us again to all of the people who have left messages for us that I have not returned. What would be the purpose in that? In hearing voices ask simple questions I cannot, or refuse, to answer? *How are you? What have you been doing? How's life?* "Interesting point," he says and nods, whenever I explain.

"Thanks for your message," I hear him say to another neglected caller in the morning. "We meant to get back to you!"

The message, I think, loving the word as I linger in our bed. *What is the message? I was a child, and then—* There I get stuck. I can't make the connection that will allow me to say, *I am myself!* Where is my self? Why can't I recognize her?

"Midlife!" the builder says, as though he's hammered a nail. But I think I am back in the loft these days because it is the surest place my body knows to find me. Of course, there are other places too, other places I would like to be, all of them in the past, which seems oddly less predictable than the future. On some mornings I feel I am not in the loft, but instead in some other unexpected ecstasy of childhood, running back and forth through wet laundry, say. Yellow and pink sheets hung to dry ripple like sails on a line that stretches the width of an ocean of grass. *I need coffee, that's what,* I think, *to get myself going.* The builder stops singing and greets me as I appear at the top of the stairs. He shouts, "Good morning, Granny!" He appears to me to be getting younger and more virile by the hour. *Poor, poor man* I think to cheer myself. Like most men, he will not realize he is dying until he is nearly dead. He suggests, tactfully, that I should do more things that bring me joy. Or that I should do some things that once brought me joy, revisit them although I am older. "Time is not terminal," he says, "and joy is not an illness. There's nothing really wrong with you except your attitude. Admit it. You're perfectly healthy. Healthy. Perfect. Joy is always possible. There's no shame in saying simply to yourself, I've been meaning to get back to you." He is so sure. So right. Where is the attitude I long for? Somewhere between sheets and sails, between the scent of cut grass and clean laundry, between what looks easy and what looks hard, between the dark barn and the loft. I picture myself rushing out onto our lawn and running back and forth between the wet bath towels we have hung out there to dry. I see not a woman who has lost her sense of joy but a woman who has lost her mind.

"You have," the builder says and laughs. "You have lost your mind."

I haven't really. My mind is with me too much. In fact, I wish it would get lost. Instead, it bullies me, delivers absurd ultimatums, transforms at inappropriate moments into a tantrum artist who flings thoughts like the hundred pieces of a jigsaw puzzle, and obsesses over mathematical equations, though I have always detested math. *How many lovers does it take in one lifetime to equal love? If you know yourself for a few years as a child, and for thirty years as an adult between, say, fifty-five and eighty-five, and lose yourself completely in the years between, when you die will you be more or less yourself?* No, my mind is not lost. But my body and its simple language of pump and flow have gone missing, so that words I once felt rushing freely in my blood drift soundless as flotsam. *Birch tree. Pipe smoke. Guitar. Lilac. Cinnamon.* I no longer know these words. In their place are prickly absolutes that sting me. You, my body tells me, will never dive gracefully from the top of a cliff into a surging river. You, my body tells me, will never repel backward, boldly, down the face of a mountain. You will no longer be tossed from the arms of one beautiful young man into the arms of another so you may sample sweet and bitter flesh; you will never bring forth a great brood of children with hair that smells of lilac, and who will play guitar for you into your old age and who will carry your ashes in a vase and plant you in the earth where you will bloom for them, a perennial mother. Your lungs are small! Your hands are shells, wobbling on the table in front of you! And your heart!

"Your daughter's heart," the cardiologist from Kashmir told my mother when I was nine and she was forty, "is funny. Not ha-ha funny, but the other. There's a hole, you see? Very common. Just a little whirring, like an alarm clock in the laundry. Not a bad thing. Unless the hole gets bigger. Then she has heart failure and kaput, she drops dead. But if it's like this? Now? Always? Then just a funny heart. Like so many. And as she gets older, of course, pain."

"Of course," my mother said.

Now my heart flutters at night, a swallow that has slammed into a wall.

IT IS AUGUST, and I am meeting my cousin Jessica in Greenwich Village where both of us once lived. I take the bus down from my place upstate and head straight for Bleeker Street to meet her in a café. We drink wine together in a sophisticated manner although once we stuffed hay into each other's mouths and flopped onto each other's stomachs in a loft. I can picture Jessie reaching her hand out to me and helping me up into the loft. Over the years, she has told me many times that people depend upon her too much, so I try to be confident and not needy in her presence. She lives now in Oregon and has children of her own and a husband who sings opera. Her tenor husband rises each day and takes a deep breath, fills his lungs to the size of gourds, and sings out the great works of Verdi, Paganini, Mozart, and Tchaikovsky. He travels to foreign countries where magnificent singing is celebrated, unpacks his suitcase, opens his arms wide, and sings. Once a year, he stays at home with the kids, while Jessie makes a trip to New York City to study fiercely for her master's degree in early childhood and elementary education. In her temporary apartment, she works faithfully at a table in a small ring of light. She reads pages of notes on childhood development, play therapy, learning disabilities, syndromes, behavioral afflictions, emotional disorders of nonspecific origins, the absence of language, the meaning of dreams, the spinning of objects, the humming of tunes, the telling of stories, the closing of hands, of eyelids, of hearts, small bodies that test the limits of all space, fragile falling selves that don't hear the adults calling. She wants to know just how we get from *there* to *here*. I'm startled when Jessie tells me that she feels anxious, restless, and unable to sleep at night. Like her life needs revision. Should she change her career? Get another degree? Move to Europe? "On my birthday, I put on black leather and rode a motorcycle. Is that like me?" she wants to know. "Or *not?*" She wants to feel joy. "I cry. I miss my mom."

Our mothers were sisters—hers an extrovert, mine an introvert—but both of the mothers are gone now, their bodies burned, and their ashes sunk deep in the earth. There's no one left to tell us about our mothers' real lives, about their fears, their choices, or about the 12,775 nights they spent lying in the darkness beside their sleeping men, the fathers of their children. We wonder if the mothers once lost themselves, for no reason at all. We wonder what dreams came to them, if any, to remind them of who they were, and we even wonder who they were, for we believe now that they were not our mothers but secret selves adrift and often empty of joy. Did they know, suddenly, one moment when they were young girls in Lambeth, rushing out the door to a dance or pushing their canoe off the shore of Lake Ontario, that they would not have long lives relatively speaking, and that no matter how far they traveled from one another, they would one day confound their doctors with parallel and nearly simultaneous deaths?

"It's funny," one mother's doctor said to the other mother's doctor, "it's as though they share the same clock. These two bodies, so different from one another, one large, one small, harboring two totally different women, one an optimist, one a pessimist, have shared a biological clock."

"Not biological," said the other mother's doctor, "psychological. Early trauma, perhaps, encoding the psyche with a shared and specific sense of limitation, exchanged between siblings bonded by a catalyst experience. An abusive father, perhaps. Or a crisis event witnessed together. A drowning. A murder. A suicide."

"Or perhaps," the first doctor posited, because he was enthusiastic about recent discoveries in this field, "early psychological trauma damaged cellular structure itself altering independent life cycles to adopt one shared rhythm."

The doctors looked down at my mother in her hospital bed, and at my aunt in her hospital bed and asked them each, "Did you and your sister share a trauma when you were children? Did you have an abusive father? Witness a crisis event? A drowning? A murder? A suicide?"

"No," our mothers said, and a few weeks later, they died.

"Don't worry," one doctor said, "their illness was not genetic."

"Be careful," the other doctor said, "their illness was inherited." Passed down through the centuries from woman to woman, like a bequeathed Chinese fan, or a pair of tiny gloves. The body is mere lace, and easily torn.

AT NIGHT, dreams repair the damage done by living. Lately, I dream I compose an opera in German, that I am a fluent and skilled librettist and composer in a language I have never spoken. I teach this opera of mine to a chorus of gifted singers who ask me questions in German as I scribble new harmonies onto the parchment in my lap. Or I dream that I write Italian elegies, volumes of verse more inspired than Dante's, or that I play the first violin in an eighteenth-century string quartet. And when I wake, for a split second I retain the gifts my sleep has assured me I possess. I speak German, I hum my opera, my fingers fold around an invisible violin. Sleep weaves a powerful self together out of exotic threads, and I am amazed at who I am, and by the gifts I might summon if only I could remember. Surely these gifts are passed down to me through the centuries, from woman to woman, out of the open space of memory where my mother wanders and her sister and their mother too, all of them looking for lost selves.

Years after the deaths of our mothers, we are still discovering objects of mystery hidden in the back of their closets beneath boards: messages scribbled in the margins of their books, bundles of unsigned poems on yellowed notepads held together with twine. In one of her mother's drawers, Jessie tells me, she found a box wrapped in linen, and inside were two pairs of tiny gloves, stiff with age, a satin Chinese fan folded shut, two garter belts, and a two-inch prayer book, a gold cross etched onto its cover. The pages were thumbed and dark. "Heirlooms" the lid of the box announced in someone's handwriting. But heirlooms passed down from whom? Maybe once long ago, a young girl—a nameless ancestor with wild thoughts in her head—sat obediently in a Lambeth church pew. She felt trapped in a starched costume. She turned the pages of her prayer book looking for some comfort as her husband stood next to her singing a hymn. Whoever she was, she has left us her prayers. And with them, I have inherited furniture, scrapbooks, photographs of houses where we all lived as children, pressed flowers from unknown romantic occasions, pipes and tobacco boxes, doilies, bell jars filled with dried leaves, Victorian valentines, glass statues of milkmaids and cobblers. I have inherited a box of wedding rings, diamond, opal, and garnet: three rings, each one removed by a daughter from her mother's open hand.

There was a party—a celebration of the opal ring my grandmother had worn for forty years—held in the white house where my mother was born, and her sister after her. Each morning for forty years their mother had woken at dawn to see my grandfather rise from his bed and fall gracefully to the floor where he performed one hundred pushups before he walked happily up the road on his "morning constitutional." The rooms of their house smelled of his pipe tobacco and of her garden's flowers. Every room was filled with party guests. My mother and her sister wore high heels and bright summer dresses and passed platters of food, while Jessica and I pushed through the crowd to reach the ashtrays filled with red-and-white peppermints that decorated the tables. We carried the mints inside our shirts and out onto the lawn, where we lay between two lilac trees that grew beside the house. A jay called from an upper branch. Its wings shook petals onto our bodies when he flew from his sweet-smelling spot. Uncle Ottmar had arrived on his motorcycle, singing a German aria.

Ottmar was an actor and a three-ring circus performer in a traveling troupe of players and stuntmen. Ottmar was family legend. He had enjoyed many wives and lovers, children and freedom, homes and travels. He seemed to pull the whole world to him with the centripetal force of his embrace, or with great circus leaps of faith and logic that show a man can fly through the air with the greatest of ease! Ottmar revved his engine in the driveway and lifted his helmet to reveal his thick white hair. "Anyone want to ride my motorcycle and know incomparable joy?"

The party went on, or commenced at last with Ottmar. He yelled and sang at its center, and told his wild stories, all of which had grand plots and dramatic endings and happy twists of fate. But Jessie and I were taken away from that drama to the room of flowered wallpaper where our own mothers had slept when they were small. My grandmother came to us there, as she had once come to our two mothers, and she placed a lit candle on the bureau where we could stare into the flame. When we asked for a story, my grandmother said this: *I've been thinking that forty years is a very long time, and I suppose I have many stories to tell after forty years. What I remember tonight is standing on the side of a dirt road in Lambeth when I was a girl. I grew up poor on a farm, and no one in my family had ever gone to school. But I did. I was the first. I went out each morning before the sun came up. The wind was bitter against my face, and I wore some rags from our kitchen wrapped around my hands to keep them warm. I held a candle my mother had given to me so I would be seen in the dark, and I had to cup the flame to protect it from the wind. And every morning, just as the sun was showing at the edges of the field, my friend, an older boy, would come along with his buggy. I could hear the horse before I could see him. When they stopped for me, my friend let me warm my hands on the horse's belly. Then I'd climb up into the buggy and go off to school, to a one-room schoolhouse where all the farm kids went. I don't know why I remember that now. It comes back to me sometimes. The wind, the way the little candle flame would dance, the sound of the horse that would take me to school.* She tucked us into our beds, and blew out the candle.

JESSIE AND I WALK together from the Village café toward the piers by the Hudson River, where kids and couples are making the most of the last week of summer and play dance music on a radio that sends voices out across the water. Everyone down by the Hudson is dancing, even the people who are alone. They move their bodies a little to the rhythms, self-consciously at first, then twirling with their hands out, their eyes wide. Some clap their hands, marking time. The air by the river smells of hot bagels and beer, and Jessie says, "We should do something wild tonight, something we'd never do, like we're young and can just do anything we want."

"Like what?"

"I don't know. Maybe get a boat? Go out on the river. We could circle the island. I've heard it's really pretty when you're not on it."

"Where do we get a boat?"

"I have no idea. I guess we'll just walk then. Anywhere. I could walk all night. I have energy. More than I've had in months. After all, when will you and I be together again?"

We cannot answer this question sent into the air on waves of music, a question that seems to be about the future but is really a question about the past. What is it that has changed? We have always parted saying, *next summer,* or *At Christmas!,* as it has always been and will always be, year after year, because we will remain women pulling our loose threads back together, reweaving what has torn, unafraid of our own unraveling selves. After all, this is what it means to remember our mothers: holding it together without them. But now it seems there is more tear than thread, more space than substance, less time than desire. It seems there is only this: Jessie walks beside me, I walk beside her. We're two ordinary women who have gone their separate ways after descending from a loft, now brushing up against one another on a New York City street, not knowing how they got from there to here.

"Do you think it's a strange fact," Jessie asks me as we approach the subway station where we will soon part, "that I have loved dearly and always only one man, the father of my children and my husband of so many years?" This is a mathematical question. How many lovers are carried within one man's body? Is it a strange fact that I, too, have slept always and only with one man who travels artfully from one lover's body to another, like a circus performer or stunt man, wondering if I will recognize him in each of his virile costumes? How many bodies can carry one man? Shall I tell her, yes, I think it is strange, or shall I tell her that the lovemaking I have known with my traveling circus lover is not joy, exactly, or not joy at all, but only its perfect lining? And what will she tell me about the life I will not lead, the life of a daughter who becomes a mother of daughters who wait for her to return across the distance?

Time is short. Traffic is heavy. The Village buzzes with light. In an instant, Jessie and I must exchange lives. I know it is possible to do this, as the physicists confirm. We have only to become two particles, two complementary natures acknowledging one another from opposite ends of the universe, each sending out to the other all the data of our existence in small losses of heat that travel at the speed of light in a mutual flash of energy, in the absence of language or of dreams. Then there will be calm and silence. This is as simple as two hands reaching across open space.

Jessie reminds me that our mothers cried and laughed aloud when their own mother died, and that they told us kids a story that seemed to fall out of nowhere. Their voices had changed as they spoke. They tossed the story back and forth between them like something light and alive, although they were dressed for their mother's funeral. There was a dance on the shore of Lake Ontario, they began. Their mother, our grandmother, had taken them there one summer to meet boys of a marrying age. There was a hotel with a wide verandah, where the young men and women gathered at dusk, and lights shone out across the lake, and five musicians played music on the lawn. My mother was sixteen, a slender beauty. Her sister was ten, tough and funny. "I wore a gorgeous dress that night," my mother exclaimed, touching her funeral dress absently, and my aunt said, "Oh, that dress! With that sequined snake on the front," and my mother said, "What a gorgeous dress, the sequins picked up the moonlight and I glittered! My dance card was filled, but I snuck down to the lake with that one boy and we sailed off in the canoe till we could hardly hear the music anymore, and we just drifted out there on the water while couples came down to the shore and danced. The moon reflected on the lake. And that boy, he recited a poem about the moon too. I'll never forget the waltz they were playing that night."

"And I never told Mother where you were," my aunt said.

"You were a good scout."

"Yes. I was. But," she added, "I really couldn't stand being left behind."

They stood for the last time in their mother's house, and then moved gracefully together in their black dresses, on their way to their places in the cemetery.

THIS IS HOW I remember my mother: not the way she looked to me when I watched her perish in a hospital gown like her mother before her, but the way she remembered herself, in the moment I believe must have been her greatest joy, as a girl drifting across a lake in the moonlight. And when she grew older, she may have seen herself the way that her sister saw her that night from far across the water—unreachable, less and less distinct in the darkness until she was invisible, dissolved into the night air. In her last years, when she slept (and like me she slept fitfully on most nights and on some nights like the dead) maybe she dreamed of dark water beckoning her, or of a young lover whispering verses to her about the moon, and woke feeling she was truly gone.

"She was a creative soul," people have said of my mother, a poet disappointed by a prosaic life. What she left behind, my inheritance, seemed so small that it went undetected for years in a cardboard box beneath her soft sweaters, a short note she composed when she was forty, twenty-four years before her death. *Goodbye, my poems, my loves,* she wrote. *I can't write you anymore. I don't know you, or myself. If I grow old maybe I'll remember you and the sound of words I once loved. Sequin. Moonlight. Waltz.*

Sometimes at night I make long lists of the things that I believe will bring me joy as I stand apart from the moments I am living. I want to walk along the shore of the Mediterranean Sea, my feet burning in the sand. I want to swim with a school of dolphins and look into one keen eye that sees beyond my body into my permanent spirit. I want to hear the poetry of Rilke read to me in the German until by the last poem I can speak the language in my sleep. I want to stand in the Sistine Chapel and look up at the hands of God and Adam as they reach for each other, and to see the divine spark of joy as it was offered by God to the first man. And where was the woman? Waiting patiently in the darkness for her own first spark of life? These things I long for could happen, but what happens first is that I leave Jessie and the city and return to my place upstate, and Jessie leaves me and returns to her place in Oregon, and no, we do not know when we will see one another again, although we have hugged one another goodbye on a street corner, feeling our small losses of heat in the embrace. "We're here," Jessie says. She turns gracefully and raises her hand. "That's what matters now."

Back upstate I swing my duffel bag over my shoulder as I walk the dirt road toward my home. I see my boyfriend, the builder, beckon to me from the high open window of the barn he is building. He has completed the outside structure, a solid design of simple lines in a European style, and now he is at work on the loft, a smaller space with only one window where he perches and grins boyishly. He looks five years younger than when I left. "Hey!" he calls and waves to me, and he points to an old ladder he has propped against the wall. "Come on up!" I hesitate for a moment, doubting the ladder, him, and myself, suspended between what looks easy and what looks difficult. I wonder if I remember how to climb—then one, two, three and up, and I am perched with him on a single board he has stretched across the open space that will become a solid loft floor.

"Wow!" he exclaims, "I didn't expect you to do that! That's not like you!"

I shrug and look out at the shadowed valley. I am not who he thinks I am.

TIME IS NOT TERMINAL. Joy is not an illness. My body and Jessie's are the solid stuff made of the dust that was a star and these bodies have circled the sun so many times. Five million years ago (a mathematical thought) two bipeds walked across a rain-swept sand, and left their footprints behind, one set moving in a straight path, the other wandering to the left, as though lost. *This,* I think, *must have been the woman,* wondering if some other way, lit by the Pleiades in the eastern horizon, might not have been the wiser path as the sands shift beneath her feet. But she returns, resumes her walk, and the man continues to sing, pretending he did not notice her wandering off like that, or perhaps not noticing at all that she went looking for herself. Again, and again, her lost self sweats and prays and dreams her into being, through words shaped by the senses and sent as a thread, a lifeline to what has been and ended, words the body whispers and which I translate now, listening to the message of my puttering heart.

Lilac. Wind. Hayloft. Lake. Mother.

What is passed down from woman to woman through the years in the guise of gloves and garters and prayer books and footprints and poems is only this, the essential self, moments of remembered joy that make it possible to live. There is my mother drifting away across the lake, where nothing but moonlight and music can reach her. There is my grandmother at the side of the road, holding her candle and waiting to learn. *Now. This. Always.* My mother was not my mother. She was water. My grandmother was not my grandmother. She was flame. I am a swallow startled by light.

End

T HE END, THE END."
The sentence is buried in the last paragraph of Vladimir Nabokov's novel *The Real Life of Sebastian Knight,* the first novel he wrote
in English. The four words appear, oddly, a full six lines before the author's last two shovels of word-dust fall, the capitalized, formal farewell:
"THE END." There's no mistaking such thumps of finality on the lid of
a narrative casket. And yet, six lines too soon—that is, before the real
end of the novel—a veil of mourning lowers and a curtain descends. We
know we'll have to leave when the lights fade and we're led offstage. The
book and our memory of its pages will leave us too one day, its details
blurred, as all things blur at the end, when we depart. After all, "The
theme of the book is simple: a man is dying." But "The end, the end"?
In the middle? So soon?

That death sentence, *"the end,"* and its echo, still stops my breath,
just as it did in 1983 when I first read it in an undergraduate fiction
writing workshop led by the now deceased novelist John Hawkes. He
had assigned the novel, near the semester's end. Did Hawkes know then
that he was dying? How could he know? The writer had years left to
live. On Thursday nights, Jack's creative young hopefuls sprawled in the
overstuffed chairs of an English grad student's living room, drank tea,
ate cookies, argued about Nabokov, and discussed one another's short
stories. Hawkes was our attentive, restless teacher. Always on the edge
of his chair, he looked ready to exit at any moment, or to fly. I remember
snowstorms beyond the windows, a radiator steaming, my own awe reflected back at me in the dark pane as I listened each week to the stories
of a slim boy, a schoolmate, Nathaniel (not his real name, of course, but
one that suits him; the real man, a novelist now in his sixties, remains
hidden). In 1983, Nathaniel's prose was already so clear, so filled with
vibrant phrases, his literary success was certain. His future filled the
room. Everyone could feel it. Like the masterworks of Nabokov's elusive

hero, the novelist Sebastian Knight, Nathaniel's fictions seemed alive. I loved them all. I hid my face behind Nabokov's book.

At age twenty, I feared that the romantic hope I felt, like Nabokov's narrator known only as "V."—a narrator I saw as similar, if not exactly like, my unformed self—would likely not be answered. I hoped to write something too one day, when things felt real. When would that happen? Would Nathaniel know? Could I ask him? And wasn't hope just busy hopelessness? Weren't hope and regret both failures of self? V. would agree, I was certain. I forgot to say *thank you* to someone who mattered; I did not praise him; we never embraced; I never found the right words. Already, I had learned one secret from Nabokov's novel *Sebastian Knight:* The train always arrives too late. Of course, I would never reach the enigmatic, talented half-kin whom V. and I admired wholeheartedly and followed for exactly 202 pages of our lives. Both V. and I had believed, mistakenly, willingly, for *two whole pages,* that a dying stranger in a hospital bed was our own lost half-sibling Sebastian, discovered at last, the embodiment of love. Sebastian still lived! We sat at his bedside, reunited. We were with him at the end. Until that is, the nurse cried out, "'Mon Dieu! The Russian gentleman died yesterday and you've been visiting Monsieur Kagan!'" Sebastian died alone. We've mourned a stranger. I held the dying book in disbelief.

But Nabokov's end is only an illusion, a conjuror's trick. His paragraph goes on, after "the end, the end." He will go on—Nabokov, Sebastian; or Sebastian, Nathaniel. I will go on as well—V. and me. "I have learnt one secret too," V. says before the novel's close. The sentence repeats itself in my ear and in my voice. Or, is it in Nathaniel's voice? Or in the voice of some other schoolmate or writer or reader I do not know? "Any soul may be yours, if you find and follow its undulations. The hereafter may be the full ability of consciously living in any chosen soul." I heard the words, then their echo. "The end, the end." Did I read it twice? Most likely I did. I curled in my bed in my university apartment, the curtains nearly drawn. I heard Nathaniel's voice. Outside, he stood beneath my window in his wool coat and unlaced oxfords, fresh-faced, amused, singing a comic lament he had written. He warbled vowels and variations of my name. I should have written down his words; they're gone. He didn't seem to care if I came to the window or not. Did he know I had just read the last page of *Sebastian Knight*? Did he know I watched him? I peeked out at Nathaniel's boyish body swaying on the front stoop. His skinny, outdated necktie fluttered in the wind. Is this memory real?

Nabokov scrawls a sentence—"The end"—on a three-by-five-inch index card . . .

Time reverses. The year is not 1983 but 1938. The place is a flat in Paris. Nabokov inhales. He has nearly completed his first novel in English, *The Real Life of Sebastian Knight*. Without pausing to doubt himself, he selects another card and draws a comma. Then, he turns the first card and writes the sentence—"The end"—again with his favorite Blackwing pencil on the card's blank side. He shuffles and flips the two cards as a sleight of hand, back and forth, and watches his little comma in motion, a half-winged butterfly. His shoulders drop, his mood lifts. He reflects on "The end." He knows how the end is always made—from movement, masked as a conclusion. He knows the end of his abandoned first language, Russian, but he also knows the start of his chosen new language, English. He knows an old world, but a new home. He knows "the end" too well in Russian; he welcomes "the end" in English—a fresh, violet fragrant phrase. "The end," he thinks, is one simple spondee, singing. He can hear that at least, though he is otherwise deaf to music. Then he performs his magic feat—with a comma, and repetition, he conjures two iambs out of the sad little spondee phrase. "Iamb," he considers. Then, "I am." And the novel's last sentence alights on his hand. "I am Sebastian, or Sebastian is I."

I was alone when I read the sentence. Am I the ones I love? Am I the ones I've lost? More than thirty-five years have passed since I first read Nabokov's novel. In that time, Nathaniel has written his own novels about love and desire, permanently extinguished by death. In his books, Nathaniel seems certain, most certain of the end. Should I write to him? Reassure him and myself? Has Nathaniel forgotten the end of *Sebastian Knight,* and those words suspended between us in Jack's classroom? Now, I continue my descent into the last six lines of my creased and yellowed copy of Nabokov's book, his first-born English child. I remember Nathaniel's voice when he sang.

"The end, the end."

Sebastian has inhaled, exhaled. He's a breath V. hears in the darkness of a hospital room. I believe for a moment I hold Sebastian's imagined form—his breathing body—in my arms, as if the creative self can ever be truly grasped. But I consider now, before it's too late, those two identical clauses Nabokov has joined so perfectly together with a comma, to form a sturdy shroud—two declaratives halved by a feminine curve. I picture two faces exposed in a one-way mirror, visible, invisible; or one dead writer, alive in the music of repetition; or one death, Sebastian's, and one memory, V.'s. Grief, elegy. Perished body, lasting art. A curtain rises. So, there is no end after all? If a book never ends, does a past? Does the day have to end on which young hopefuls sit together in a room with their teacher, reading stories? Or must we all go our separate ways? Snow falls, the radiator steams. "The soul is but a manner of being. Any soul may be yours if you find and follow its undulations." Nabokov's "The end, the end" offered a joy I'd never before considered, a phrase for the "interchangeable burden" of all losses. Each life inexhaustibly departs, ad infinitum, and there are so many ordinary last words repeated throughout a life, cried out from one hospital bed or another, at one graveside or another, in friendship and farewell, sung by a young writer beneath a window and dissolved as quickly as "stone melting into

wing"—yet all of these transformed by one tiny mark, a comma, made by
Nabokov's Blackwing pencil that keeps all weak hearts beating.

Now, to "animate the past"—Jack asks me in the last year I see him
alive, "Did you like the book I gave you? Did you like *The Real Life of Sebastian Knight*? Will you pass it on to someone else?" He asks as though
the novel he has bequeathed to me will continue its journey through the
unlikeliest of students. Six lines under the sentence, "The end, the end,"
in Nabokov's final passage of the novel, is a truth he wants his grieving
narrator V. to see, or maybe, the truth that Jack wanted me to see, or to
see himself before he died. A book survives and speaks from the grave.
And who can know if it's a real truth worth believing until the final,
faded page seems done? There is no period after

THE END

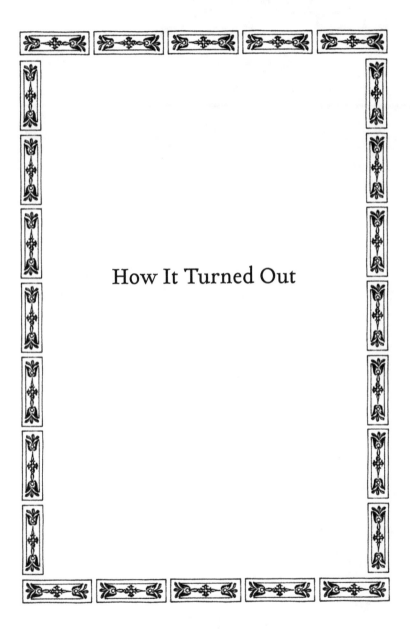

How It Turned Out

I REMEMBER IT WAS *raining that night.* The streets were empty. I was on my way home. I had to get across the city and then travel north to my apartment in an old building between the train tracks and the river. From my apartment, I could hear the trains speed through at night and see the ships move by during the day. I planned to board trains, ships, and planes one day, to get away from everything finally, when I had money. Get away from what? Maybe my mother. Inconveniences. Maybe something else I hadn't figured out. I didn't have much money, I never did, so hailing a taxicab that night was *out of the question.* A taxi would have been the safe choice because I was alone. There were few lamps on the avenues back then. The city was dimly lit forty years ago. I saw red and green reflections on the wet pavement as the traffic lights flashed their instructions for English-speaking pedestrians to either Walk or Dont Walk, no apostrophe. Every now and then the beam of headlights from an occupied Checker illuminated me, alone, in my raincoat. Otherwise, the streets were dark. Beneath my coat, I wore a white spring dress. Maybe I had been at a party. Maybe I had taken myself out to some East Side movie house with my few dollars. Three dollars and fifty cents seemed like a lot back then. Maybe I had attended one of those free bookstore readings by an author I liked. As usual, I did carry a hardcover book under my arm. I should mention that last night, I stayed up too late watching news reports and old television shows, and this morning, these thoughts came up and took me by surprise.

I wore high-heeled shoes. The shoes were favorites of mine and I had no difficulty walking in them. Forty years ago, I walked easily, without worrying about my bad hips and my bent feet. I didn't worry I might tip over without warning, like I did last night. I had gotten out of bed for a drink, the left hip just gave way, and I fell over sideways onto the floor. I lay there briefly on the rug, startled to be there. The cat stared at me from the bed while I got back up on my feet. But years ago, when I still lived in the city, walking was an easy means to an end, and a pleasure. I walked almost everywhere even at night, though my mother had warned me not to do that. I was only twenty. I thought, if my decisions weren't good, so what, I had lots of time to learn. My body was slender and nimble. I had a swing in my step, even in the rain. I had slim ankles, no hips, and a small bust my dress suited well. My hair was dark brown then, and hung down to my waist. That night I wore it pulled back, secured with a rubber band. I glided along like those trains and ships I longed for. At the corner of the avenue, the red light flashed Dont Walk. I stopped obediently at a safe distance from the curb. My mother had warned me once that a car might spin easily out of a drunk driver's control, crash over the curb, and disable or kill pedestrians, and the image must have stuck with me. There were few cars that night, but the city felt menacing. I was all alone in the white dress. I shouldn't stand there by myself. I should keep moving. A bus stop was blocks away.

A voice called, "Excuse me, Miss?"

Halfway down the block behind me, a man rolled. He waved at me. He sat in a chair, tilted slightly to one side. Quickly, he dropped his waving arm back down over the side of his chair, and rested his hand on the wheel. He stopped rolling a few feet away from me. His black hair fell damp across his forehead. He wore a brown leather jacket, one sleeve draped loosely over his shoulder, the collar turned up around his neck. I noticed right away that he was a very thick, muscular man, and I tried not to look directly at him. My mother had advised me that one should not look directly at disabled people, it was rude, and I believed her. Actually, I couldn't remember seeing disabled people in the city at all, except the homeless ones that pedestrians ignored in the streets or in stairwells. The man rolled even closer to me. I stepped back.

"Yes?"

"I'm sorry to trouble you, Miss, but would you push me?"

I tried to make sense of him. "Sorry, what?"

"The chair," he said and smiled. "I usually get around just fine, but it's raining and to tell you the truth, I'm tired as hell. I have a few more blocks to go to my hotel. Do you mind pushing me there?"

I minded. The situation seemed inconvenient at best, risky at worst. After all, it was just him and me on a dark empty street. He looked large, even in the chair. I looked around for someone who might be out walking their dog, just taking a quick spin around the block with a poodle, someone older who might offer to help me. My mother had told me that this is how young girls wound up in the back of a van, bound, gagged, and overpowered by a duplicitous actor, a man posing as someone a young girl would pity. *Never trust a man who tells you he's "disabled,"* she said. Wasn't this situation exactly how I would meet my end, disappear without a trace off a city street on a rainy night?

The man looked directly into my eyes. I didn't expect that! He rolled himself backward a little and left more space between us. "Listen," he said. "I'm a pretty strong guy, but I'm tired. I've been waiting for someone to help me. And here you are."

"Well," I said. I didn't want to be rude. He was so friendly. I could say no to him, politely and emphatically, but then what? Wait for the traffic light to flash Walk and take off at a sprint? Leave him to sit there by himself in his chair in the rain? He couldn't just hop onto a bus. Forty years ago, the city buses didn't even have lifts and ramps, nothing was easily accessible, and I couldn't remember when I'd last seen the Handicapped Access image of a person in a wheelchair, just like this man. He would have very limited options. My mother would want me to say no to him, I thought. She would say, *Get out of there! For god's sake, haven't you ever watched a movie or read a book?* My mother would want me to run as fast as I could away from this man who was tired in a chair. She was probably right.

"How far away are you going?" I said.

"I'm staying at The Drake for a few nights while I'm in town. You'd do me a good turn if you'd say yes."

At least he had named a hotel I knew existed, even if I'd never seen it. The hotel's name seemed like a purposeful detail I was meant to weigh favorably, and I did. But it might be a trick. I tried to remember, was The Drake Hotel in this neighborhood? Probably. Most of the good hotels were somewhere near the park, and that wasn't much farther. And whatever happened, at least we'd be headed toward a busier neighborhood, with bright lights, maybe some after-dinner traffic, hotel people departing and arriving, taxis loading and unloading passengers.

"How far away is The Drake exactly? I'm in kind of a hurry."

He paused and shrugged. "Three or four blocks. Not too far."

"Okay," I said. "I'll push you."

The man seemed unimpressed, but said, "I appreciate it. And I'll hold your book for you while you push me." He held out his hand as though we might dance. His hand was quite wide. I gave him the novel I had been carrying. He glanced once at its spine, shook the tassel of my bookmark a little and then lifted the book twice beside his shoulder to acknowledge the volume's heft. He winked at me and tucked my novel inside his leather jacket, which looked to have a fleeced lining. He pulled his jacket closer around his chest. "If your book gets rained on," he said, "the pages will be ruined, and then you won't find out what happens next. You've already gotten so far."

"True," I said. "I could get an undamaged copy somewhere. Thanks, though."

My face hot, I stepped behind his chair and began to push. The chair seemed ridiculously heavy at first, I recall. Who the hell makes these things, I wondered. The man's chair was just a metal box that had to be forced up hills, no motor. No wonder he wants someone to push him, I thought. But once I got the thing underway it wasn't so bad. We rolled over to the curb's edge. The curb was the hard part because forty years ago in the city, all the curbs were high and sharp, dangerous hurdles designed for hurried pedestrians to conquer routinely every three minutes or so as they dashed across the city to their destinations. I tried to tilt the man's chair backward a little. I didn't want the chair to lurch. I didn't want him to fall out onto the street or to feel a bump that would bother him. Could he feel anything? I wondered. Was he completely paralyzed from the waist down? I peeked over at his thighs and they definitely looked okay, long and blue-jeaned—from what I could see of them. He said, "Just go for it. I'm all battened down." The traffic light flashed Walk and we bumped down the curb, and I saw him stiffen in the chair for a moment. Going up on the other side was even harder, but he turned a wheel to help me so we went up and over the little cliff together, and then we repeated that process at each curb after. One clunk down, two clunks up. We were headed for The Drake Hotel. That's what I hoped.

It rained harder. I pulled my hood over my head while the man talked to me over the sound of the rain, and we moved along the streets. Periodically, he wiped his eyes and brushed streams of water off his jacket. When a motorcycle sped by and sent up a noisy wave along the sidewalk, he raised his hand over his face. His jeans were soaked black. I wished we would get to The Drake immediately, which—it soon became obvious—was not a few blocks away at all. The trip was much too long. We were not going to the hotel, I realized. When we reached the seventh or eighth block and the man was still pointing ahead and saying, "The next one, keep going," my nerves were shot. I wished I'd said no to him, and felt bad about it. Maybe he would soon stand up from his chair and confront me with the truth. The man said, "Hey, I guess the hotel is a little farther away than I said. But you might not have pushed me if I had told you how far away it was, right? You never know how people are going to react to the chair. The weather isn't great."

"It's not," I said. "That's okay."

"So, I take it you're a serious reader, huh? Me too. Why don't you tell me about that novel you're reading, since I'm wearing it right now and there's still a way to go? What's the plot? Any good characters?"

I don't remember the plot of the novel now, but I do remember that I told him what had happened in the story so far. Over the top of his head, I described for him each of the characters and their apparent and hidden motives, as well as I understood them, and some of the settings that seemed interesting or like they might prove to be important later. He asked questions and prodded me for more details and descriptions. He seemed genuinely curious.

"Sounds complicated," he said. "I love complicated novels. Do you like Russian literature? Now that's complicated stuff! My favorites. Subtext is everything, I think. A real gold mine for an actor. I read a lot of novels now, more than I used to. I started reading young, did you? I read because I wanted to be good at my job, the best. Reading was a big part of it. Reading all those scripts, finding the meaning inside the stories and making them feel real to other people, making characters really *matter*. I like to make things matter. How about you?"

"Absolutely," I said.

"I'm a communicator, always have been, but especially on the screen, I mean. I was a good visual storyteller and that wasn't just about my face, or my voice and the sentiments, but because of my physicality. The body is an actor's instrument, you know. It tells you a whole lot you need to know about a person, sometimes even more than what they say. People could relate to me, back then. They could really see me. That was important if you wanted a name in the business."

"What sort of business?" I said to keep him talking, so I wouldn't have to pitch in anymore. He talked into the rain. My throat was sore from the damp, my ears ached, my feet had actually started to hurt and slip around in my beautiful shoes that I loved so much and that were now stretched and ruined! But, I could see lights and the billowing flags at the hotel's entrance up ahead. There it was. The Drake Hotel, for real. He hadn't lied to me after all. The whole experience was almost over. Soon I would say goodbye to him and have to go to my apartment.

"Movies," he said. "I was a screen actor. I am. You wouldn't know me. I mean, you wouldn't recognize my name. I never made it big because of the accident. That really put a kink in the whole plan. But I was pretty good in the '60s, a contender you could say. I worked a lot. TV stuff, detectives mostly. I got the lead in a big film, top bill, good production value—lots of money, good director, great cast—but no. Drunk driver. No more big deals for me. I went a different way."

"Looks like we're finally here," I said.

"We made it! Good job."

"Good evening, Sir," a doorman at The Drake greeted us. "Good evening, Miss." Quickly, the Doorman opened one of several doors so we could roll into the lobby of the hotel. The lobby was long and smooth like a frozen lake with a carved front desk. Small lamps hung from the ceiling and cast a warm gold light. There were a few chairs arranged neatly around the draped walls, with people chatting in them. No one looked up when we came in, drenched.

"Just take me over to the front desk."

"Good evening, Sir. And Miss," the front desk clerk said, and looked at each of us. "Awful weather. So sorry."

"All good. We like rain. And Russian novels. Don't we?"

I nodded. "Yes," I said. "We do."

We parked his chair, and I stepped in front of it. I stood as near to him as possible, by the tip of his leather boot. I extended my hand. "It was nice to meet you," I said. "And really nice talking with you."

"You too," he said. We shook hands. His was incredibly warm and rough. He tipped our two hands gently to the right, unexpectedly, so I took mine back and hid it in my pocket. I tried to read his face. "Thanks for the push. Please don't be insulted, I don't want you to be, but may I offer you some payment for your effort? I know it was a longer trip than you expected. We're both soaked. And I did lie to you."

"Oh no, thanks, that's okay," I said without moving. "I didn't mind."

"She didn't mind." He smiled and slicked his wet hair back from his forehead. He pulled thoughtfully on his earlobe for a few seconds. I felt that he might say something else to me, he looked like he was going to, but he didn't. I stared at a tiny smudge on his cheek, a curved moon-shaped mark just under his left eye, like a fingertip had touched him there. Now that we were in the bright light of the hotel lobby, I could see that his eyes were dark blue with very long lashes, and that he was an unshaven, rugged man, forty-five or so, old but somehow still fit like a former athlete. His face was lined and weathered, and was the kind of face my mother would have said was *roughly chiseled* or *well lived in*. I wondered how long ago he'd had his accident, exactly how long he'd been sitting in that chair.

"Hey, don't forget your book," he said suddenly. I had completely forgotten he was carrying my book. For a moment, the sudden intimacy of his gesture as he reached deep inside his jacket confused me, and then I remembered, I *was* reading a book, I had told him the whole plot of it too, or as much of it as I could without knowing the end, although I can't even recall its title now. I wish I could remember. I might still have it somewhere on my shelf. The cover of the book felt hot from his body when I held it again. "I hope it has a great ending," he said. "You let me know how it all turns out." He told me his name.

"I will," I said. "Have a good night."

I hurried out of the hotel. I had to get away. I slipped once on the lobby's polished floor, but I recovered from the stumble. I hoped he hadn't seen! I hugged the book in both my arms, against my breasts. The Doorman wished me a good night as I went past, and offered to hail a cab for me, but I told him no, I wanted to walk. Actually, I wanted to run, to make myself sweat, breathless, to board a train or a ship, or to fly off high over the city, and of course I had no money, a cab was *out of the question*. I don't remember what happened after that or even how I got home. Was it still raining or not raining? Was it a brightly lit street or a dark avenue? Was I near my home, or still miles away from it? Should I go back to the hotel? Would he be sitting in the lobby still? What were his private movements, alone in his hotel room? Would he make a late-night phone call before he slept? Would he take a hot shower? Did he move easily from his chair into the bed, between the sheets? Read a novel? What book was he reading? Had I read it too? What was the name of that film he was almost in? Was he happy? Did he miss acting? Had he been a good actor? He must have been. Who would remember him? Why was he in the city? How much longer would he stay at The Drake Hotel? Did he always stay there when he was in town? Who touched that moon mark beneath his eye? Whom did he want to hold when he got home? Where *was* his home? And what would happen when he returned to it?

THAT'S IT. That's the whole story. Almost the whole story. Or, just what came back to me suddenly when I woke up this morning after my late and restless night. It's missing something, I know. But you can't include every detail. You have to choose. Sometimes, you think a story's going one way, and then it goes another. Or it just gets away from you. Sometimes things don't turn out in the end the way you'd expect. For instance, I forgot that whole episode for the rest of my life, until today; the night we talked and moved together along the dimly lit avenues through the rain came into my body again, unbidden and alive, forty years later. I've wanted to write what I remember. But it's possible that the beautiful Drake, demolished years ago, may not have been the hotel that I recall. We may have been in some other hotel lobby. Or maybe the weather wasn't all that bad, I'm not sure. I can't tell which of his words and mine are both a truth and lie. I'll never know why our paths crossed that night. And the only absolute facts I won't include are these: First, that after I pushed him to his hotel, I opened the book he had held safely for me inside his jacket, and discovered a fifty-dollar bill tucked between the pages. Second, that a few days later, I found—in a 1960s screen-actors' magazine—a youthful image of him smiling, wearing a hat. I returned the fifty dollars to him in an envelope I took to the clerk at the front desk of the hotel. The clerk told me *the gentleman checked out*, but he would certainly get my note if I wanted to leave it for him, he was a regular guest. I printed his name on the outside of the envelope. On the inside, I included the money and a card on which I wrote, "No problem. Happy to have met you," and signed my first, middle, and last names clearly, and underlined them, for whatever reason. And lastly, that ten years or so after the night with him in the rain, after a half dozen moves from one place and job and man to another, I received an envelope in the mail, addressed to me in unfamiliar handwriting. Inside the envelope was a page torn from a movie script. On it were fragments of dialogue between two characters, but I could make no sense of them. "You pushed me a long time ago," someone had written across the side of the page with blue ballpoint pen. "Never forgot. Thanks. Take care." I guessed it was a message from the past, and when my boyfriend asked me as we stepped out for our evening in the city, who was that letter from? I answered with certainty, "Some guy I pushed in his wheelchair."

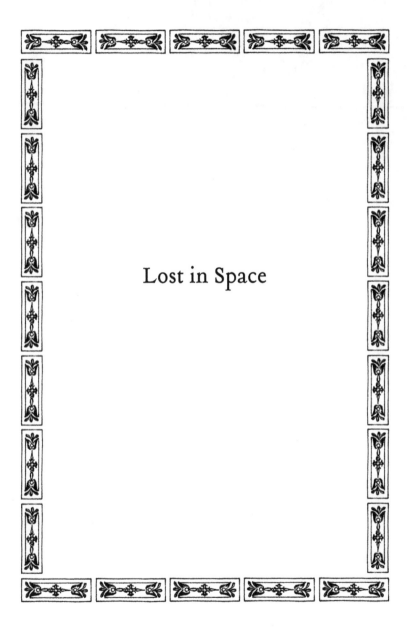

Lost in Space

THROWN FROM ITS trajectory by a meteor storm, the *Jupiter 2*, a small, spoon-sized saucer of a ship that contained elevators, long corridors, control rooms, and multileveled family quarters, traversed the galaxies hopelessly off course, for years. Would the Robinsons—a space colonist family of five, John, Maureen, and their three children Judy, Penny, and Will—ever find their way in the *Jupiter 2* to their new home, a planet near the galaxy of Alpha Centauri? Or must they return to the Earth where they began? Aliens, giants, walking vegetables, and space monsters aligned against them. Doctor Smith, the cunning stowaway, did his utmost to lead the family to their doom. Would the Environmental Control Robot warn young Will Robinson in time of the unexpected dangers, its lights blinking like a Christmas tree, its spherical head spinning and pumping up and down in mechanical distress? "Warning! Warning!" I shouted to my father in imitation of the Robot when it waved its Slinky-like arms in the air. I waved my arms in the air too. "Ignominious ignoramus!" my sister said to me, playing Smith's part. "You lame-brained lump! Pusillanimous Pipsqueak!"

"Shush," my father said, patting the two of us back down. "Watch what's happening. Wait until it's over."

"That does not compute, that does not compute!" I said in my best Robot voice.

"You're going to miss all the important stuff!" My father flopped down on the center of the bed, more eager than we were to watch the week's episode. I tucked myself under his right arm. My sister tucked under his left with her Bunny Puppet. I was four; she was seven. I could not see her over the broad expanse of our father's chest. He smelled of soap, sweat, and wool. That scent, and the rough wool of his sweater against my face, are the first details I recall of our weekly TV ritual— watching Irwin Allen's sci-fi adventure *Lost in Space,* or *L.I.S.,* as my father called it fondly. "Kids, time for *L.I.S.!*" he yelled for us when he arrived home on those evenings. He kissed my mother, and then went straight to the Emerson. From 1965 to 1968. Three seasons. Black and white, for us. Every episode. Our three bodies pressed reassuringly together, my sister, my father, and me. Through all the endings of suspense, as the Robinsons once again headed toward their doom. The image on screen would freeze at the worst possible moment of their latest ordeal. What could possibly happen to the Family Robinson *next*? Would they survive?

"A *cliff*-hanger?" my father exclaimed in mock disbelief.

Words flashed across the screen in answer.

"To Be Continued Next Week! Same Time Same Channel."

THE FACES OF THE Robinsons appear to me now fifty years later, as I remember my father. In 1965, when the first season began, my father was forty years old, and actually looked a bit like Professor John Robinson, or, like the actor Guy Williams (known to some as *Zorro*), himself forty-one. Both of them were trim, dark, and their hair was always disheveled despite their efforts to slick it back—a problem, maybe, of gravity. Williams never acted again after *Lost in Space* went off the air—apparently, he flew to Argentina after the last episode, and did not return to the States—but for a while, my father and Robinson seemed twinned in their white T-shirts and high-waisted trousers, their belts cinched tight. I knew they each had the tough job of being captain of the ship, but John Robinson seemed to have the harder time of it. The threat of lightning storms, quicksand, missiles, and time warps kept Robinson always in a light sweat as he scouted the terrains of unfamiliar planets with his family huddled in the back seats of the space chariot. Miraculously, there was always oxygen to breathe, but his radio often failed from cosmic interference, and the alien ground seized and shook with unexpected thermal upheavals. Nevertheless, Robinson always reassured his trembling children. "Now, we're all going to be without gravity for a while," he would explain casually, "so we better hang on"; or as their ship slipped hopelessly toward the sun, "In a matter of hours, we're going to be in danger of roasting alive. There's no time to get back to the ship, we're going to have to build a shelter right here." Maybe my father admired the man's obvious finesse in tight spots, or hoped to fashion himself after his look-alike Robinson, a brave pilgrim of the future. I am surprised to notice now in photos of my father as a boy—sandy hair combed neatly in a bowl cut and his lower lip slightly pouting—that he also once looked exactly like young Will Robinson, transported in time to 1935.

Of course, my father's universe in boyhood was a much smaller one than Will Robinson's—just a few short streets of pool halls, a hardware store, a smoke shop, a movie theater, and a penny-candy counter at a cinderblock gas station in a failed coal mining town in Pennsylvania. Daily after school let out in summer, my father ran beside the river, past the baseball field, past the graveyard where his relatives all lay buried beneath brown grass, past the plot of earth that was marked already for him. In one photo from that time, he wears a crisply pressed sailor suit, although there was never a ship in sight, and he looks directly into the camera with a solemn gaze. He sits beside his father. Doc's fleshy hand rests firmly on the boy's bare knee. The gesture appears benign and possessive at once. That hand, I imagine, pressed down on my father throughout his life, and held him inside to a place he wanted to escape. How far was he willing to go? He enlisted in the army. He changed his first name, and shed "junior" permanently. He traveled through three countries in two years. He considered moving to Indiana, or Ohio, then landed in New York with my mother where he finally had children of his own and watched *Lost in Space* in the evenings with them like the family man he had determined he would be. When he settled in to cheer for the Robinson family, he seemed to my sister and me more like a big kid. Did he imagine himself soaring beyond the Earth in the *Jupiter 2* at a calibrated "perfect escape velocity"? Might it have been the Robinson son he watched and rooted for so faithfully, and not the Robinson father? When he watched *Lost in Space,* did he see the son and father together as two resilient versions of himself, boy and man, traveling together through time?

When I watch *Lost in Space* now, I see in the first season the serious ambition of the show's writers. They offered a TV show of the future that pitched a plausible physics, a new frontier in space, but that also regularly paid homage to older fantasy narratives. The show drew adventures and tropes visibly from the science fictions of Wells and Verne, Jack Finney, and John Wyndham, yes, but also from Victorian fairy tales, Norse mythologies, medieval legends, Shakespeare's *The Tempest,* and Bible stories. Fittingly, the show's episodes were all over the place, careening among their source materials, albeit dependent mostly on the lodestars of Virgil and Homer whose epic tales of Aeneas and Odysseus—their blackened vessels tossed and wandering upon the seas—foretold John Robinson's future odyssey in deep space. In voice-overs, Robinson narrates his adventures in the tradition of the ancients. Alas, the special effects of the show, like craft projects, seem silly to me now. The meteor storm that tosses the spaceship looks like a handful of granola tossed at an Altoid; the Robot resembles a Shop Vac; the space suits that once looked to me so shiny and impressive, featured even in fashion magazines of the '60s, now look right for a Zumba class. These details are to me as charming as the Robinsons' prevailing trust in honor, virtue, and in each other. Certainly, the Robinsons are a very unlikely family. Daughter Judy clearly has Nordic roots, daughter Penny uses a breathy, British inflection, son Will is all-American, a heartland child. Only Penny resembles her parents. Nevertheless, they do all speak—and shout—similarly; that, is, *very slowly,* even as they shoot their lasers, dodge rockets, confront extraterrestrials, and sink deep into galactic quicksand. How is it possible for actors to be both lethargic and urgent simultaneously? The cast manages it, and this now seems right to me, actually even inspired, because this *is* what it feels like to be truly lost:

Urgent Lethargy steers your ship. I am startled to feel that the show is strangely relevant now, and may be in any era. In the episode "The Stowaway," a President of the Future (1997!) deeply laments the over-populated Earth and the dying environment, as most presidents do. The Russians manage to sabotage the ship's course at launch. The flecked paint swirl of the cosmos depicted outside the viewing deck of the ship and inside the lens of the *Jupiter*'s telescope strikes me as a strangely authentic metaphor for hope. Most remarkably, the actors of *Lost in Space* throw themselves into every far-fetched scenario without a cringe or a blink of irony. Instead, they look at one another with trust and love, the prevailing values of *L.I.S.* Through the force of their will, the Robinsons still command our attention. Our respect. Our loyalty.

My father gave them all of this fully, for three seasons.

He followed nothing else on television in the 1960s as far as I know. For a long time, I believed my father was a dedicated fan of science fiction. He did own a two-volume vinyl recording of Orson Welles's infamous radio broadcast *War of the Worlds,* but in time, it became clear that his enthusiasm was only for the genius of Welles, and not for the Martian invasions. A few years after *Lost in Space* surprisingly beat *Star Trek* to the coveted network spot, that other show finally surged into popularity and it seemed that no one cared much about the idealistic *L.I.S.* anymore, except my dad. The crew of weird trekking isolates aboard the starship *Enterprise* bored him completely—he preferred the wholesome Robinson family, whose tight-knit family allegiance eclipsed every threat in outer space. I am not sure to what detailed extent *L.I.S.* was indebted to Johann David Wyss's 1812 novel *Der schweizerische Robinson,* the tale of a Swiss family, also named Robinson—Wyss's own backward nod to *Robinson Crusoe*—shipwrecked in the East Indies after seriously losing their way to Australia in a storm. I do not believe my father owned that book as a boy or had any special interest in novels about the Swiss. I *am* certain that the opening of each *L.I.S.* episode—scored with orchestral brass and woodwinds in a buoyant tune composed by young "Johnny Williams," who would later define the sound of fantasy cinema—must have thrilled my father's ear for music. He would be delighted, surely, by the opening credits that featured simple cutout figures of Robinson, Maureen, and their two daughters arranged in an animated collage, the four of them tied safely together by a rope as they galloped happily through the stars. What could possibly be better than *that*? my father must have thought—*did* think—throughout his life.

Does an explanation for my father's love of *L.I.S.* hide in his life story? He should tell the story himself, although it is one that he never wanted to tell anyone in much detail, except in small bursts of anecdote or anger. Sometimes, he mentioned men we never knew, fellow soldiers who had traveled with him across England, France, and Germany until the war's end; or a place he had once enjoyed as a boy—a theme park, an ice cream shop, a baseball field beside the Allegheny River. Sometimes he mentioned an insult that he had endured and carried with him across decades; or rolling with his benumbed unit into Marseilles at dawn after a three-day pull without sleep; or a rare surprise trip to Philadelphia he had once taken long ago on a train with his father, just before his parents' terrible divorce. He seemed to have saved few artifacts of his journeys. One Christmas when my sister and I were still children, my father did pull a large box out of storage and unpack for us eight metal cars of an old electric train. "My father gave this to me when I was a boy," he said in apparent disbelief. My sister and I joined him on the floor where he sat cross-legged, in deep concentration, carefully hinging all the cars back together and laying the metal track in an oval on the carpet. When he hit the switch, the first time he had done so in decades, the train lit up—we all cheered!—and the cars lurched into a slow whirring motion. After decades in suspended animation, the train resumed its journey. In a way. It traveled *backward*. The caboose pulled the engine in the wrong direction, and then stopped, despite my father's repeated flicks of the switch. My father packed the train back into storage, where it remains to this day.

Nevertheless, I have now inherited abundant mementoes of my father's life. Open boxes of his letters, his medals, and his photographs surround me. On army stationery, and in small black-and-white snapshots, he documented his journey with the Twenty-Sixth Special Services Entertainment Company in World War II, from 1943 to 1945. He recorded his observations of people, the ruined cities, and of the larger military operations as he understood them at eighteen. He found himself in charge of the entertainment for the Twenty-Sixth, and in tents along the route often played music and projected reels of black-and-white films for the men. He was responsible too for driving through dozens of deep-night landscapes while the other soldiers slept in the back of the vehicle. *Swindon. Newbury. Perrier. Eisenberg. Bensheim. Erlangen. Munich.* In July 1945, he wrote, "Homeward bound. But *when?* They keep saying soon, soon. Then *nothing.*"

In a photo I took myself at the Veterans Day Parade in Manhattan in 2014, he grins atop the World War II float, his arm raised to the cheering crowds as he sails along happily. In the older snapshots I scrutinize, I can see the tall, slender soldier that he once was, standing alongside a barracks, or pouring gasoline into a six-by-six, or perched on a tractor in a barren field, or leaning in the war's aftermath in full-bodied relief against my smitten mother.

Maureen Robinson is the only character in *Lost in Space* whom I now find impossibly outdated. This is not surprising. Identified as an astrophysicist when the *Jupiter 2* launches, Maureen enacts mostly domestic duties in space as the series unfolds. Accompanied by a gentle oboe theme, there she is—perfectly coiffed with strategic curls that frame her face, her bow-shaped mouth thick with lipstick—carrying a white plastic laundry basket. She sorts the Robinsons' towels and napkins. She instructs Penny and Judy on the proper planting of peas in alien soil. She explains the first stirrings of sexual desire to a disgusted Penny, who has glimpsed her older sister practicing the art of flirtation, which prevails even in other galaxies. "Well Penny, dear, young people sometimes have ways of doing things that may seem a little *strange*," Maureen tells Penny sweetly while John smiles at such carefully chosen words. He kisses Maureen later with passions of his own.

That current of desire between Maureen and John—or was it between June Lockhart and handsome Guy Williams?—seems genuine. Desire fills the void of outer space with an electric energy I never noticed consciously as a child, but that must have been more than evident to my father. Did he heartily approve? "I've got to get back to the ship!" Robinson says fiercely whenever he strays too far from Maureen. With Maureen, Robinson concludes every triumph over danger with a lingering sensual kiss, and then, a big hug for the kids. Without Maureen, who registers on her heart-shaped face the reality of danger, the burden and depths of her worry—No water! No food!—the Robinsons would cease to be a family facing the loss of one another. Robinson's mission, I see clearly now, is to hold his family together, to secure them to one another, perhaps, with a steel tether. As a result, every episode has the same predictable plot: Judy saves Will; John saves Penny; Will saves John; Penny saves Will; John saves the children; the children save their parents. I always loved it as a kid when Maureen finally shook things up and showed her stuff. She grabbed her space helmet, threw on her jetpack, hooked herself to the side of the ship, and swam through space to reach poor John Robinson, accidentally untethered from the *Jupiter 2*, and floating away from them all—until Maureen hauled him back to port.

Unlike Maureen, my mother would not have boarded the *Jupiter 2*. She feared travel, and for the entirety of her life could not bring herself even to sit in an airplane, despite the opportunities, so great was her terror of flight. After my sister and I were born, my mother took only one journey with my father. I remember them standing together, his arms wrapped around her on the dock before they boarded the *Queen Elizabeth II*, the ship that would carry them to England. She waved their tickets above her head, and looked up at my father with absolute trust, but I am certain she was frightened. When they returned from the journey, they both seemed deeply relieved to be back and they told no stories of whatever sights they had seen. I have to imagine them on the ship as they once were, in love beneath the crescent moon. I imagine they stepped out onto the deck, hand in hand, to admire the sea in a rosy-fingered dawn. Maybe they looked through the telescope and spotted a blackened wooden vessel disappearing over the ocean's edge; or maybe they just gazed toward the stars flung far above them, shining in the distant galaxy called Alpha Centauri.

Desire fills the void.

In a box of ephemera, I found the two creased QEII tickets my father saved, along with dozens of hand towels from every locale where he and my mother had traveled together, including the House of Lords.

WHEN *LOST IN SPACE* went off the air after three brief seasons, television rituals with my father ended. So did that particular kind of early closeness that my sister, my father, and I had shared. Whatever the tether was that secured us all together, eventually unraveled, and our long drifts apart began. After they did, I do not recall my father watching much television again for over forty years, until he was in his eighties. By 2016, the small apartment where we had all lived together had been my father's, alone, for over two decades. My mother died in 1994. My sister flew that same year to land permanently on the West Coast, another galaxy. I moved upstate, where I routinely left one town and relationship for another every few years, and—with only a few possessions, the supplies necessary to pretend a settled life—my time passed at the speed of light, and not at all. I stayed connected to my father by phone. I sent him weekly reports, or sometimes I traveled back into the city for a visit with him. I watched him get smaller, though undefeated by age. Sometimes he looked deep into my eyes. Other times, he seemed not to see me at all. In the evenings, he shuffled down the hall between the rooms that his family had once filled and that now overflowed with all the possessions of his ninety-one years. In one room, objects were stacked so high a window was no longer visible. No light came in, no breezes. The place was dim. The radiators clanked and spewed steam. The climate often seemed uninhabitable, but he did not want to leave. He fell silent when anyone suggested he move on to an assisted living facility or to any space more benign and navigable for a man of his age. His will, it seemed, was inexhaustible. Pure power of mind held his ailing body together. Gradually, I understood that my father needed not only to live *in* his own space; he lived *for* it. His home—his idea of home— kept him alive.

I sat down beside him in the oppressive dark. We watched TV together again.

He lowered himself cautiously into his favorite winged chair in front of his new flat-screen television. He clutched the TV remote in one hand, his cell phone in the other. He alternated turning the TV volume up and then down with his left hand and answering the phone with his right. He worked the controls. My father and I watched football, mostly, and game shows. He watched as though he had never seen a television before. He became an obvious admirer of a game show hostess. He knew the answers to all of the questions on *Jeopardy!* He sampled the show *Mad Men*, but only once. "They all drink a lot," he said and shrugged with irritation. "Nothing interesting ever happens." Instead, he surfed the stations looking for old classic films, always hoping to see Orson Welles magically appear. He was largely disappointed. The only series I believe he followed for a while was *Desperate Housewives*, but the crush he confessed to having on the housewife who bears a mild resemblance to my mother soon overwhelmed him and he had to stop watching. Surprisingly, he showed no interest in family dramas or in science fiction. His youthful loyalty to the adventure of *Lost in Space* had been unique, a quirk of mood inspired in him by the mood of the 1960s, or by his children, or by something else.

Maybe, after all, *Lost in Space* just meant a lot to me, and nothing to my father. That is possible, I suppose. When I hear the opening theme of the show, I still feel a sudden surge of joy. I look forward to something—who knows what?—although my habit is to travel backward. Was there joy for him, with us—with my sister, and me? I think so, but I will never know for sure. Possibly, when he arrived home, my mother met him at the door and looked at him with desperate eyes that begged him to allow her a moment to herself, away from the children. Could he give her that? Could he just *take them* so she could have one hour alone to play a record she loved or make a phone call, or even to weep a little in the kitchen over a burnt meatloaf she had yet to master? She was completely exhausted. One hour, or even a little more? Please?

Was *Lost in Space* my father's gift to my young mother?

Silence stretches between us now and yet my father's voice remains perfectly clear to me, without any cosmic interference at all. He still sounds in my head just the way he did in 1965 when he lay in front of the TV, and kept my sister and me close. He whoops and cheers as the Robinsons' space chariot, with John at the wheel, heads boldly toward an inland sea the family must cross together. My father yells at the television, "Yeah! Keep going! Do *not* turn back! You can do it!" He squeezes us and says, "Do you think they're really going to make it, kids?" I twist the wool of his sweater and squeal. I hide my face against his arm, place his hand over my ear, and then peer out at the television again, enthralled. I remember the sudden rise of waves, the black sky and the black water indistinguishable from one another. Wind spins the space chariot and lightning strikes the waves. The Robinsons, drenched, toss around together inside their tiny ship, which heads toward a whirlpool, a Charybdis that pulls the sea into its vortex and then spews it out again. Will Robinson shouts. Judy sobs. Penny sobs. My sister and I scream. Robinson pounds on the controls as they head toward the abyss. What is he *thinking?* Maybe he sees himself as an ancient seaman—a born navigator, a survivor—who will rebuild his ship every time it shatters. After all, he slid into the catacombs beneath an avalanche of galactic ash, and he escaped! A rampant king controlled his soul, and he escaped! He staggered and fell paralyzed in an electrical storm, and still, he escaped. True, he concedes, lost in thought, the family is in some trouble, but he wants only to dance in his space boots with Maureen, kiss her pink-bow lips, and secure in her hair a flower plucked from the soil of a fertile planet.

My father yells loudly at the TV screen. "No! No! There's no *power!* Goddammit, there's *got* to be more power! Keep going!"

As though he has heard a voice in the currents, or a distant dispatch from Alpha Central Command, Robinson looks up wildly. He flicks a switch. The space chariot surges forward past the vortex, and my sister and I clap and cheer as my father pulls us to his chest. "See, kids?" he says. "They made it! Again! We didn't worry, did we?" The episode draws to its close as John Robinson writes peacefully about the ordeal in the ship's log. We hear his final words. "We have passed through the fury of the inland sea. We are now safely encamped in the spaceship, at least momentarily secured from the extremes of heat and cold as well as the violent molecular storms that characterize this remote and unidentified planet. The supreme question now is whether we can *survive.*"

To Be Continued Next Week.

"Same time!" my father says.

"Same channel!" my sister and I chime.

AFTER THE MEMORIAL SERVICE, my sister asked me "Do you remember when we used to watch *Lost in Space* every week with Dad?" We are both middle-aged now, and on the few occasions when we are together,

I find it difficult to picture the two of us as we were in the 1960s—tiny enough to fit our bodies entirely beneath our father's arms. "I do remember," I assured her and for a moment, we stood together. Then, without speaking much, we began the long work of sorting through all his bequeathed belongings. We stuffed them into garbage bags. We hauled them down to the street, delivered them to charities, and to the recycle bins of *Got Junk?* We distributed the most precious items among relatives and friends. We divided the letters and the photos. I took down all of the old draperies and the gates on the windows that my father had installed decades ago to bar all invaders and enemies. Two hired men arrived, and with sledgehammers, they finally got the family sofa out the front door. I shredded and recycled the carpets. Wrapped the mattress in plastic. I found a small painted carving my father had made by pounding on wood with a cut-off ten-penny nail when he was a little kid—a perfect yellow house with open shutters nestled beneath a blue sky. An ideal home. I also kept a wool rug I found rolled up in a blanket in his closet. "Guess who made this?" he had asked me once, spreading the rug proudly across a table. "Not bad, huh?" The soft yarns he hooked himself long ago depict a rolling ocean, and at the center, a ship with sails unfurled. I sorted through all of the pictures he had sent back on his one road trip across the United States in his station wagon, the Maid of the Mist. He had loved to drive the rusted Maid. He swore she would get him across the country, and she almost did. He had booked a flight back. There were images of Mount Rushmore, Pike's Peak. Mesa Verde, the Grand Canyon, Yellowstone Park, with my father standing proudly in the foreground of the landscapes, his eyes shaded behind sunglasses. On the back of each card and photo were his brief travel notations: *Two more weeks, then home. Home in one week. Three days left, and then, Home! At last! Tomorrow! Flying home!*

We boxed up the dozen stuffed animals we discovered he had saved on a top shelf of the cabinet for over fifty years since our childhoods, and we shipped them far away to needy kids in Africa—or so the charity worker promised—except for Bunny Puppet, which my sister reached for in grief.

IN 1968, *Lost in Space* was canceled without notice. After eighty-three episodes, the station did not renew. None of the actors, the writers, or the viewers ever found out what happened next week. The story stopped in the middle as the family wandered a planet of ephemera that they had barely explored. So, all of the questions remain.

Were they lost in space forever?

Did they ever find the galaxy Alpha Centauri?

Did they finally make it home?

I think of my father's last day on Earth. He knew when he woke up in a hospital that it was the end. The nurses tried several times to place an oxygen mask over his face to ease his breathing, but he pushed them away. "It's over," he said. "Don't any of you know that? It's over."

He had just enough breath left to cry out two words.

Home. Now.

In the empty space where my father once lived, I found a last object left behind. In the kitchen closet, hanging on a yellowed two-by-four board among dozens of rusted keys, was a plastic key chain: a tiny replica of the Robot from *Lost in Space,* its arms outstretched as if to me.

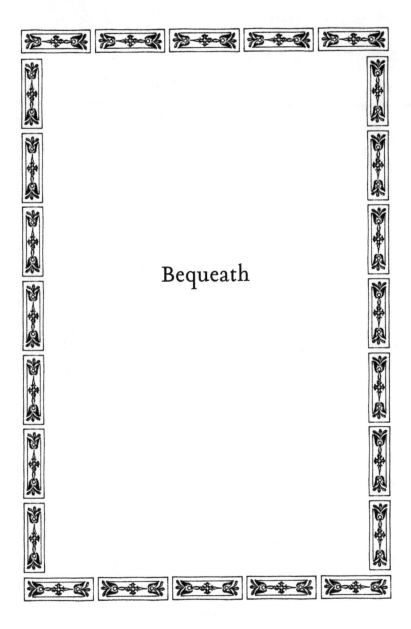

Bequeath

HIS WILL WAS A STANDARD ONE, prepared, witnessed, and signed over twenty years before he died at the age of ninety-one. He named his offspring, my sister and myself, as coinheritors of all his savings and property, which included a co-op apartment in Manhattan, and the contents of several small bank accounts. But in an unexpected prose paragraph on page two of the Will, he left his car to me, and his piano to my sister. After the apartment, the car and the piano were his two largest possessions. Next in size would be his saxophone and his clarinet, which were not listed in his Will but were the objects we associated most intimately with our father, and with his voice, now quiet. My sister wanted to have the clarinet. The clarinet in its small black case would be best, too, for her to carry on the plane back to the West Coast after his memorial service. I wanted to have the alto sax, his first instrument, his last instrument, the one he'd discovered as a fifteen-year-old boy in 1940, and played in the army Special Services in World War II, and then in clubs in and around New York for the rest of his long musician's life.

The clarinet was my father's second horn. He had learned to play it when he was twenty-three, after the war, to keep his place in conservatory, where talent for merely one instrument was unacceptable. The clarinet became his choice of second instrument. I haven't asked my sister if anyone has played my father's clarinet since she boarded a plane with it six years ago. His saxophone hasn't been played once in the years since he died and I brought it to my house in upstate New York. It remains in a cool closet. I've had the saxophone cleaned, of course, polished professionally down at Cole's Woodwinds, where Cole or one of his several sons said, "It's a good horn, a classic. Take care of it." The sax is still ready for music, but I don't expect to hear it again. In silence, I remember its sounds perfectly, the deep notes my father played through all the years of my childhood and my adolescence. I wait for the *right* person to play his alto, to breathe into it, with no luck. I'm drawn still to the sound of the instrument, so I toss money to buskers, who nod as I pause to hear them play. I linger for hours in clubs and bistros, nursing drinks I don't really want while I listen into the wee hours to a stranger play notes that take me back to my father, or bring him back to me. *Moonlight in Vermont. They Can't Take That Away from Me. Manhattan.* My father travels across time and space on the tones of any alto saxophone I hear, on tunes played by anyone at all—skilled musician or amateur, vintage chops or mint—while I get drunk and dizzy.

When we saw his two bequests in the Will, seated across from one another in our lawyer's office, my sister and I exchanged a look. We felt inconvenienced. We saw difficulty. These two items—car and piano—seemed like burdens. Why direct these possessions directly to each of us? We'd inherited them anyway. Maybe my father had thought to himself, well, one daughter wants a car, and the other daughter wants a piano. And that was true when we were little girls, and even later, at the time he wrote the Will. But when he died, it was no longer true. I was fifty-four years old. I no longer needed a car. I had my own used Corolla with low mileage and a CD player in the dash for playing Van Morrison, Sam Cooke, Johnny Clegg. My sister no longer needed a piano; she had a Casio, a used keyboard well-suited to her apartment. In a sense, we had already inherited someone's car and piano. What mattered, though, was what my father meant at the time he wrote the Will. Embedded in the bequest, there was a message. Did he want his daughters, in our different ways, to feel free? To move and to be moved? To improvise? Did he want us to press the pedal and go? Maybe he had watched his two daughters thoughtfully for years, and knew what medicine we would need most after he had died. When my sister and I were kids, on weekends we had played a game with him in the Metropolitan Museum of Art. My father would hand each of us some clues he had composed on scraps of paper. "Louis XIV collected these, because he really liked to sneeze." Clues like that. He set his daughters loose in the museum's marbled halls to play detective. Each object he chose for our investigation had a unique history, a meaning we had to pursue and discover, on our own. Maybe he still wanted us to play, after he was gone.

The car I inherited was a beige Ford. A Taurus, like my father. The Taurus was the last in a long line of his cars that had met assorted fates: The Green Dragon, The Lemon, The Maid of the Mist, and Grandma's Buick. The Buick had been crushed by a boat at a traffic intersection. The Ford sedan, with its large trunk for his horns, mics, and amplifier, was also a last generation of the Taurus before it was terminated by the Ford company. Could such a great car just disappear? My father took good care of the Taurus. Maybe they shared an understanding. He had respect, too, for New York City's alternate-side-of-the-street parking regulations, and would never let the Taurus offend the city. He parked his car on the Upper East Side streets, and moved it every other day, a habit he had maintained with all his cars for forty years. Even in his eighties, he maintained the strict routine. He wanted to keep the car "active," as he put it. Usually, he fell asleep behind the wheel while he waited in the early hours for a parking spot. When his neighbors left for their work and noticed my father in his car with his head tipped back and his mouth fallen open, they thought many times that he had died, in the hour of departing souls. In my father's ninetieth year, after he played his last gig, the tenant in apartment 4A—a detective for the NYFD sympathetic to my father's old age—parked the car for him in a safe precinct downtown. His car had not been taken away; it was simply well parked. He could live with that for a short while. After he died, the Taurus waited for him to move it again beyond the bardo of Canal Street, but that task would be mine. On a fall morning six months after my father died, I grabbed his key chain, a plastic replica of the robot from *Lost in Space*, and took a train downtown to find the car. The Taurus was easy to find. On the dashboard were the protective NYFD tags. After a brief fumble, I found the key and turned it in the ignition. Nothing. Silence.

The piano my sister inherited was a Sohmer & Co. brown upright.

The apartment was a third-floor walk-up, and delivery or removal of the piano—of *any* piano—should be memorable but I recall only that, in 1967, there was a sofa where my mother lay on her stomach reading novels and then, magically, the upright piano stood in the sofa's place. There was a storage bench, in which my father kept sheet music, show books, Fake books, band charts, and classical portfolios. Quickly after its delivery, the piano became the center of attention, our family hearth for years. On holidays, friends and relatives stood around it to sing while my sister played carols, show tunes, and movie songs. With our cousins, we sang all the songs in *Oliver!, Anything Goes, Chitty Chitty Bang Bang,* and *Wonderful Town.* My uncle, virtuosic in any key, accompanied my mother and her sister, who sang duets—"Chattanooga Choo Choo," and "Don't Fence Me In." They crooned, "Why, oh why, oh why, oh why did I ever leave Ohio"? Together in resounding voice we all sang "Seventy-Six Trombones," from *The Music Man,* and with my dad at the piano, we kids belted out "The Wells Fargo Wagon / a comin' round the street"—a song about a wagon filled with strange items to bequeath: maple sugar, grapefruits, a bathtub, raisins from Fresno, a cross-cut saw, a salmon, and something called a grey mackinaw. Was it a bird? A canoe? I pictured the majestic mackinaw. To make his daughters laugh, my father at the keyboard kept repeating the tune's final chords as though the song would never end: "It surely could be something special / somethin' very, very special now, just for me! / It surely could be / somethin' special / somethin' very, very special, just for me! / Oh yes, it could be / something special—," on and on. No one manufactures Sohmer pianos anymore. Back in their day, they had the sound if not the status of a Grand. They were called *the poor man's Steinway,* or *the Piano-Maker's Piano,* which meant great craftsmanship, great sonority, facts that mattered to my father. I like to believe that Hugo Sohmer—a cherub-faced sixteen-year-old piano maker's apprentice in Germany, where my father's own family began—designed my father's upright piano himself. Or, that Hugo at least imagined the *possibility* of my father's future piano. The tone. The deep resonance. The gold third pedal for sustaining sound, "the soul" of the piano. And especially, the passive aliquot strings that vibrate in sympathy each time the hammers hit the others. Hugo got the patent for them, finally, in 1880. His pianos gained international respect. Did my father's upright—made in Sohmer's New York City factory in 1925—have the aliquot strings? After my father died, I looked inside the piano and noticed a small plate affixed at the harp, with Sohmer's name engraved on it, as though Hugo—and all his sons and grandsons, the "& Co." who inherited Hugo's business across a century—still lived inside the instrument.

There were no other pianos in the building's apartments. In 3A, an artist painted blizzards in oil. In 2A, a cab driver left the TV on all day. In 1B, an editor raised two cats, Simon and Schuster. In the apartment directly below ours, 3B, Handsome Pete deplored pianos with fury. He was unimpressed with our musical efforts. He was not charmed by children. He did not appreciate Broadway show tunes. *Chitty Chitty Bang Bang* drove him nuts. He phoned to complain. He rang our doorbell, repeatedly. He yelled insults into the air shafts of the building. When my sister and I continued to play piano, he pounded on the door of the apartment with his fist. Once, my mother opened the door to reason with Handsome Pete, to explain children, practice, and enthusiasm, and she was so overwhelmed by his grand beauty and his startling resemblance to a piano with his black brows and moustache, white teeth, and ivory-colored suit, she only nodded as he raged. Pete smiled when he said, "If you don't shut those dear children up I'll bring a hammer and an axe up here, beat this door down, and chop that fucking piano into smithereens!" I loved that new word "smithereens." Fantastic! My mother nodded. She said she understood. She closed the door, and wilted against it. She said, "Why does he look like *that?*" and after a pause, "Wouldn't an axe be sufficient?" My father laughed. He wasn't scared of Pete. In retrospect, Pete's threat doesn't even seem that odd, merely of its 1960s era, when artists chopped up pianos in concert halls, for audiences, as "Destruction Symposiums" and "Destruction Happenings," duets of piano and axe performed on stages in London and New York, for Pete's sake. Confusingly, many times as a kid I'd heard my father call his own saxophone The Axe. *"Me and The Axe play tonight at ten!"* Axe, I discovered—thanks to Handsome Pete—is both endearment and threat, music and madness. Artlessly, Pete did beat on our door one day with a heavy object. Boot or bat, pipe or hammer, we never knew. The object left pale bruises in the paint. Our door, if nothing else, was scarred. Finally, HP moved away. Half a century later, the piano remained intact, but no longer in use. In 1994, the year my mother died, my father had shut the fallboard. The neighbors never complained again. He piled novels on top of the Sohmer, then tchotchkes, wine glasses, photographs, cassettes, and CDs. Old sheet music, wooden recorders, and a half dozen Hohner chromatic and diatonic harmonicas—artifacts from my twelfth year when I had longed to play the blues harp like Little Walter—rusted in the piano bench, along with a harmonica holder like the one Bob Dylan used, but broken. When my sister cleared off the piano, her inheritance, and opened the key lid, the embossed name of Sohmer & Co. still shone in dignified gold script. The ivory keys had faded. I said, "I think it's illegal to sell ivory." She struck a few of the keys. The piano was not badly out of tune.

YEARS PASS AS YOU sit at the piano. When you are seven years old, you climb onto the bench. Your feet dangle above the pedals. Your hands are too small to play good tunes. You can't reach across an octave. You look up at the music on the rack. You count measures. You have a new "Very First Piano Book." Your teacher has assigned the first tune in the book. You have a week to learn it. You practice it to perfection for your father. *Tony the Pony.* C D C—D E D—C D C D—E D C. Four measures.

One line. Repeat. You never forget Tony the Pony. He is slender and gray, and his long soft nose rests on the fence. C D C. You love Tony. D E D. Tony is gone. You're playing *Buzzing Bee* now, with both hands at the same time, it's a miracle how fast your fingers fly! You understand "staccato" and "allegro," "presto" and even "prestissimo," and you buzz across the keyboard from one blossom to another, playing the bee's swift flight, its changes of direction, its rest in the shadow of a petal. And then *Buzzing Bee* is a faint insect whirr of the past. Your father says, nostalgically, "Play *Buzzing Bee* for me again, why don't you?" But you shake your head "no." Classical music swells. The low notes of your left hand play undercurrents of meaning beneath motifs articulated by the right hand. Your fingers curve above the keys. You press the pedals with your agile toes, muting and releasing sound. Your whole body plays the piano now. In the music of *Für Elise*, you hear romantic turmoil, a struggle between a man's admiration of a woman and his more urgent longing, and so the right-hand notes speak of trivial matters and the left-hand notes speak with passion. Elise says No. You feel pulses of joy that shake the air. Suddenly, your body feels warm and wild. You've entered the Rag Time, Real Time, Best Damn Time with Scott Joplin, your new hero, the King of Ragtime! Your teachers don't approve of your romance with Mr. Joplin. Oh, come on, why? They must hate that syncopation that makes you wiggle on the bench. How can they not like, not even get, *Maple Leaf Rag*? They prefer Bach, Stravinsky, Debussy. Your father gets it and he's on your side. He says, "It's all connected. You swing, Fastback!" Gradually, you surrender to your adolescence. You sing laments. You play pop ballads by Neil Sedaka, Billy Joel, Jim Croce, the Carpenters, and Barry Manilow that leave you wrecked and lonesome. And when you learn it's true, breaking up really *is* hard to do, even if you're just a teenager, you slam the lid of the piano bench as hard as you can onto your open hand. You don't find it hard to do. You don't find your decision strange. Crushed, your hand and wrist swell, purple.

You cannot play piano for weeks. The music you made can be unmade, so swiftly. Music comes, it goes, you have it, you lose it, you need it, you fail it. Music of love and pain.

HE LEFT THE CAR TO ME. My plan was to drive the Taurus upstate and park it in my driveway. I'd place a "For Sale" ad on the local paper's website. The car's estimated value was four hundred dollars. But it wouldn't start. I waited on Canal Street for a tow truck. The street was busy with traffic. The sun was surprisingly bright for November. I sat for an hour alone in my father's car. The upholstery smelled of him in his old age. A beaded cushion, flat and misshapen, covered the driver's seat. The worn cloth upholstery cushions and the compartments contained dozens of small items he had left behind as clues: expired and unexpired ID cards, weird broken plastic objects, a stuffed wolf, a tiny sombrero on a string, a half dozen air fresheners shaped like Christmas trees, several pairs of clean tennis socks and two canisters of tennis balls. He had not played tennis in fifty years, despite the wins of his youth; in his final year, he cut fresh tennis balls open with a kitchen knife, and attached them to the metal legs of his walker. He hated the scrape of metal on pavement. I found malted milk-ball wrappers, too; a yellow Matchbox car; folded programs from Yankee Stadium, The Big Apple Circus, Radio City Music Hall; napkins from the Café Carlyle jazz club where his idol Bobby Short no longer played the Steinway baby grand; and a half-empty bag of Spangler's Circus Peanuts, orange chewy banana-flavored marshmallow things my father loved, inexplicably. The Peanuts, invented in the '40s, had outlasted my devoted father, their creator Arthur Spangler, seven successor sons, and two grandsons, who bequeathed the Spangler Candy Company to the fourth generation. But the Peanut recipe never changed. Sugar, gelatin, corn syrup, and artificial color. Recipe of survival. Now, the Company advertises Peanuts as a candy of "Nostalgia." I recalled that as a boy, my father had lived near a penny-candy shop, where his love for sweets began, and that even in letters he sent home from France during the war, he'd asked his mother only for warm socks and boxes of candy—"licorice and chewy thingamajigs." Before one year in the army and his nineteenth birthday had passed, my father had lost all his teeth. He wrote home to ask then not for candy but for a Brilhart sax mouthpiece, the best, like the one Johnny Hodges favored, and Lester Young.

I stared at the yellow sign he had taped inside the Taurus's passenger window: NO RADIO. I put the sign, and the other items into a garbage bag. I sat with my hands on the steering wheel. The mechanic who arrived, finally, to meet me on Canal Street with his tow truck had a cheery attitude about the Taurus. He rested his hand possessively on the car. He said, "It's a good car. Not much wrong with it. It needs a new starter." I said I understood, and asked him if he'd like to buy the car for two hundred dollars. He said, Wow, yes, that would be a big help, he had kids. We agreed to meet that afternoon again, to complete the sale. By midafternoon, I no longer wanted to sell the Taurus to the mechanic with kids. I sent him a text. He didn't reply. I removed the license plates bearing my father's name, put them into my tote, and called another tow truck. A new mechanic came, less friendly than the first, who towed the Taurus to a different garage and scrapyard near the Hudson River. I rode along in the truck's passenger seat, looking backward every now and then at the Taurus dragged mutely behind us. When we arrived at the garage, I met the garage owner. I asked him if he would like to have the Taurus. He said, "It looks like a good car. Good shape. It's got some years. You sure you want to leave it?" I said I was. We shook hands. Behind him, the Taurus was ascending already on some sort of metal lift alongside several other cars, most of them bent and badly damaged. It occurred to me these cars soon might be crushed for the scrap yard. "What will you do with the car?" I asked the garage owner who looked, suddenly, irritated. He shrugged. "It's not your car. What do you care?" I took a last look at my father's Taurus and walked uptown.

WHEN WE WERE KIDS, my sister and I played duets. We sat together on the piano bench. We wore identical striped dresses with strawberry pockets. We lifted our hands in unison. We played "Chopsticks." "Heart and Soul." *Pachelbel's Canon. Ode to Joy.* We shared mistakes, and fixed them. Practice is repair. Our father said, "don't practice your mistakes or they'll become the tune." The last song my sister and I played together was "Joy to the World." "Jeremiah was a bullfrog, was a good friend of mine!" Our father backed us up on the alto, adding sax riffs that rocked. "Singin' joy to the world!" we were a real trio. "Joy to the fishes in the deep blue sea!" My sister and I wouldn't hear that song again until the church organist played it reluctantly and gloomily at the memorial service. Then my sister and I went our separate ways. Two ends of the line.

From her coast, she wrote to ask, what are the dimensions of the piano? From my coast, I responded with the needed four measures: Height: 52 inches. Width: 62 inches. Depth to soundboard: 14 inches. Depth to keyboard: 27 inches. She asked, what is the manufacturer's serial number? I answered, can't find it, or just missing. She designed a donate webpage; I took the photos. I photographed the piano in various lights with its fallboard closed, and opened. I photographed the piano from different angles, at midday and at dusk, in natural and artificial light. I arranged sheets of music artfully across its rack. I got close-ups of its keys, and of its name: Sohmer & Co. New York. The piano looked attractive and well made. It might catch the eye of a charity, church, or school. It could be someone's perfect match. When the match was made, however, more questions would arise: How would the piano get from the top floor of the building down to the sidewalk? Who would carry it down three narrow flights of stairs? Would the piano damage walls, the steps, the men? What about lawsuits? How was it delivered when my father had purchased it in '67? The tenants in 3A, 2A, and 1B were long gone— the painter, the cab driver, the editor. As audience, they might have had some useful memories to share. It didn't matter. The high schools did not want the Sohmer; the churches didn't either. The Donate to Educate locations in New Jersey, Long Island, the Bronx, and Brooklyn, all passed. The folk café did not need it. The Unitarian Preservation Hall already had two pianos they didn't use. Only the world remained. And when my sister asked me, "Do you want it?" I did, and wrote back to her immediately, "That's not practical for me."

The apartment emptied, slowly, of all its furniture and artifacts. Objects went in various directions to new lives or appropriate ends. Upright and silent, the Sohmer watched everything go, until it stood alone. The final plan seemed clear. Professionals would dismantle the piano, "dismantle" being, of course, a vague word. A relationship can be dismantled, or an argument. A good reputation can be dismantled. Even a life's work. A score and a text may be dismantled and reassembled, repeatedly. Such dismantling is quiet, methodical, and subtle. Sometimes, a habit may be dismantled. For two years in my thirties, I dismantled beaver dams on the flooded land of a farm. I tugged at the tangled twigs, vines, and unyielding branches. I hacked at them with a hatchet. I dug into the packed mud for hours, until I was exhausted. Every morning, I found the creatures had repaired what I'd destroyed. In darkness, they reconstructed what they needed, without a flaw, over and over, like perfect practice. Everything back in place, exactly the way it had been. It was in their nature, or their memory. *This* dismantling, I feared, would be very different. I expected the dismantling of the Sohmer would be in the desecration style, a Destruction Happening, the bequeathed upright piano crushed on both sides, the faded ivory keys stripped and sealed in bags, strings severed, the intricately carved mahogany lid and legs broken and splintered in every direction, and the delicate gold plate bearing Hugo Sohmer's name, affixed within like a heart, unsalvaged. Nothing would be left, not to anyone. The men would wield the heavy tools their job demanded with an efficiency their company assured, just like Handsome Pete had promised, back when my sister and I were kids. "Smithereens," he'd said. And I had loved the word.

I SAW MY FATHER seated alone at the piano only once, when I was young. He didn't know I watched him. He was slumped forward in his T-shirt and khakis. He squinted at some sheet music he'd opened on the music rest. He played simple chords and sang softly, figuring out a new song for the horn, for later. I hadn't heard my father sing by himself before. He had a gentle baritone. The song had a refrain I've always remembered, "Have I stayed too long at the Fair?" There was a catch in his voice. I felt I'd discovered something secret in him, something I should never mention, no matter what happened, and I never did. Without a sound, I left the professionals to their task. I removed myself, as though I played no part in loss. And when I returned to the empty rooms after the dismantling was done and the men had packed their tools and hauled the remains of the piano away, it seemed that nothing momentous had occurred. Nothing irreversible. Nothing permanent. No crescendo, just silence. The piano vanished as simply as it had appeared fifty years before. The wall where it had stood was vacant. My father was gone. I didn't see the axe fall, I didn't hear the hammers hit the strings, but there were vibrations for many years.

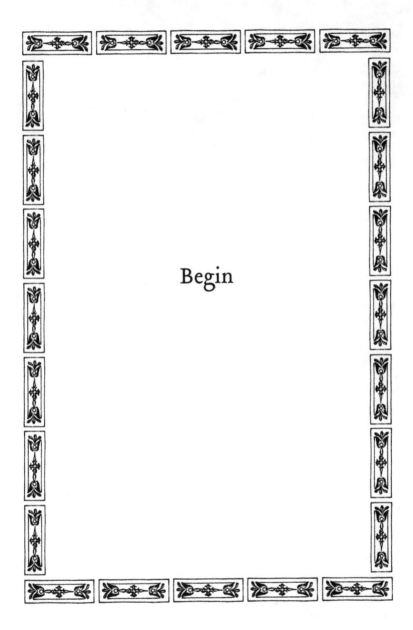

Begin

I SAT, MY MOTHER'S arms around me, the large book open before us. The volume was held together with a frayed twine we unraveled together, as though the book was an ancient gift, its giant pages askew and unglued by the touch of forgotten hands. The cover was a faded shade of yellow—and on it, a boy was flying! Words ran in ribbons at the bottom of each illustrated page. Every picture was a rich, deep color. I saw dark-blue starry skies, and dark-red feathers, and that boy with bright cheeks wore a lush green hat tilted jauntily on his head. And there was a small fairy, with pink skin and golden hair, and the most delicate pale-blue wings rising up from her shoulders. I don't remember hearing my mother's voice as she read aloud, or the details of the many illustrations. But I remember very well turning to a particular page that became the first page of my life. Suddenly, I was staring at a painting of myself or of some part of myself that I didn't yet understand, but felt unfolding, vivid and mysterious, within me. I couldn't breathe. The picture moved.

The boy's eyes are wide. His red lips are parted in a gasp. He looks down at the small, stricken fairy. Between her delicate hands, she tips a goblet of poison to her lips. I can see her wings moving a little as she drinks, the tiny blue veins woven like threads inside them, keeping her aloft. She has small breasts and slim hips. Her wings, I see, are the sum of her. She hovers in the air beside the boy's open mouth. He could swallow her, the two are so close! She can feel his breath on her body. My skin is hot and tingling. Am I afraid? No, but what else could feel so much like fear? My mother still holds me, she's reading aloud, but there's a thrumming all around me. I study the soft flesh of the fairy. Everything she feels is so obvious to me, so visible. This is a picture of love. I hear the boy cry out to her, "O Tink! Did you drink it to save me?"

"Yes."

Of course. She loves him. She doesn't want him to die. He is her best friend and more, too, though they are of different, distant realms. What good are her wings, anyway, without him? *Drained it to its dregs, drained it to its dregs,* the words stir the air. He watches her drink with disbelief, alarm, and possibly horror. This is a picture of anguish. Do I only imagine that her form is reflected exactly in the blue pools of his eyes, as though she lives and dies inside them?

"But why, Tink?" he asks.

How strange that he asks her this second question. What in her deed does he not understand? He is no longer asking why she drank the poison; he is asking if she *loves* him. Isn't her love—isn't *all* love—apparent? Doesn't he know? Maybe she hid her light from him until now; maybe she had been only a breeze around him, a nearly imperceptible humming he could not name, her vibrations strange to his senses. Maybe his disbelief explains why he is alone, still sewn only to his own shadow. This picture of love makes no sense, and perfect sense: she has spent herself entirely on loving him, and now he knows the truth.

Most everyone who has ever been a child knows exactly what happens next in this story, except *I* don't yet know because I cannot leave them. If I could, I would soon find out that he rises to the occasion of her deed. He summons the world to her repair. If you believe in fairies, he will explain to all the readers of his story—and his story is now her story too, or it has always been—she won't die. If you tell her she is real, she will be real. He can turn this loss around, with his will and his desire. If you believe, clap your hands.

But his passionate act, and the noise that erupts as riotous reply in all the earth's innocent nurseries, happens on the *next* page, the page I haven't yet turned to in this book that has been bequeathed to me. I remain as small as a fairy sitting in my mother's lap while she reads to me—*drained it to its dregs, drained it to its dregs*—a girl lost in a book, bereft and excited at once. I gaze at the two of them. They are so beautiful, and of such separate species, each of them now exposed to the other as their eyes meet over the cup. My mother squeezes my body to make me breathe.

She doesn't know what I have seen.

Maybe she does.

Before she opened the book, and before I entered this picture, I did not know that love is a deed; that it must be gulped like a poison, or like a wine that either kills you or makes you fly up on wings toward the mouth of your favorite human being; that the beginning of a story may look like the end; or that the future is a draught poured in a heavy goblet you must lift, somehow, to your own lips—because there's no other way—not knowing if you will survive the act or what may happen next, only that something must, something will, if you believe.

ACKNOWLEDGMENTS

I am grateful to the editors of the following journals, in which these essays first appeared, some in other forms: *Brick* ("Fall of the Winter Palace"; "End"; "Begin"); *Crab Orchard Review* ("Poison Hour"); *Fugue* ("Joy"); *The Normal School* ("Masters in This Hall"); *Salmagundi* ("Lost in Space"); *Southern Indiana Review*/Thomas A. Wilhelmus Award ("Mystery Girls"). "Masters in This Hall," in different form, is anthologized in *Every Father's Daughter: Twenty-Four Women Writers Remember Their Fathers* (McPherson and Co.); "Fall of the Winter Palace" is anthologized in *The New Brick Reader* (House of Anansi Press). My professional thanks to Jay Rogoff, Phillip Lopate, Margaret McMullan, Claire Messud, Susannah Mintz, Greg Hrbek, Steven Millhauser, Michael Ondaatje, Jim Shepard, Tara Quinn, and David L. Ulin. My appreciation to The Corporation of Yaddo, MacDowell, the New York Foundation for the Arts, and Skidmore College for awarding nonfiction fellowships and grants. Thanks to Ashley Gilly, Catherine L. Kadair, Michelle Neustrom, Sunny Rosen, and James Wilson at LSUP. Special thanks to James W. Long, Senior Editor at LSU Press, and to Susan Murray, for their expertise and guidance. Thank you to my friends who read, consider, and support this work. My loving thanks to Nick. For my godparents Libby Sherrill and Bill Kaufmann, my love and gratitude always.

* * *

PERMISSIONS ACKNOWLEDGMENTS

W. S. Merwin, excerpt from "The Present" from *Garden Time*. Copyright © 2016 by W. S. Merwin. Reprinted with the permission of The Permissions Company LLC on behalf of Copper Canyon Press, coppercanyonpress.org. Reproduced with permission of Bloodaxe Books, www.bloodaxebooks.com. @bloodaxebooks (Twitter/Facebook) #bloodaxebooks. Used by permission of The Wylie Agency LLC.

The Wells Fargo Wagon
from Meredith Willson's THE MUSIC MAN
By Meredith Willson
© 1957, 1959 (Renewed) FRANK MUSIC CORP. and MEREDITH WILLSON MUSIC
All Rights Reserved.
Reprinted by Permission of Hal Leonard LLC

Joy To The World
Words and Music by Hoyt Axton
Copyright © 1970 IRVING MUSIC, INC.
Copyright Renewed
All Rights Reserved. Used by Permission
Reprinted by Permission of Hal Leonard LLC

Ohio
Lyrics by BETTY COMDEN and ADOLPH GREEN
Music by LEONARD BERNSTEIN
© 1953 (Renewed) by CHAPPELL & CO., INC. and LEONARD BERNSTEIN MUSIC PUBLISHING CO., LLC
All Rights Administered by CHAPPELL & CO., INC.
All Rights Reserved
Used by Permission of ALFRED MUSIC

Z
·フ C

Printed in the USA
CPSIA information can be obtained
at www.ICGtesting.com
CBHW021606200924
14723CB00002B/118

9 780807 182772